instant **expert** • instant **expert** • instant **expert** • instant **expert** •

BEADING

Thunder Bay Press
An imprint of the Advantage Publishers Group
5880 Oberlin Drive, San Diego, CA 92121-4794
www.thunderbaybooks.com

Copyright © MQ Publications 2005
Text copyright © Lucinda Ganderton 2005

Series Editor: Katy Bevan, MQ Publications
Editorial Director: Ljiljana Baird, MQ Publications
Photography: Lizzie Orme
Styling: Catherine Huckerby
Design Concept: Balley Design Associates

ISBN 1-59223-344-9
Library of Congress Cataloging-in-Publication Data
available upon request.

Printed in China
1 2 3 4 5 09 08 07 06 05

BEADING

lucinda ganderton

THUNDER BAY
P·R·E·S·S

San Diego, California

Contents

INTRODUCTION

One of my earliest memories is of sitting at my grandmother's kitchen table with my sister and spending long hours playing with the family bead box—threading, counting, stringing, and sorting the glittering array of faux pearl, glass, plastic, crystal, and Venetian beads that had accumulated over the years. Each one seemed to have its own character: a smooth, green oval that resembled a grape; a mysterious orange scarab; gaudy, swirly, hand-painted wooden beads; somber Victorian jet drops; and—my favorite—a faceted, pewter-color, art-deco necklace.

I've never lost this complete fascination with beads and still find their decorative qualities irresistible. They are versatile, gloriously colorful, readily available, and can be sewn, wired, threaded, knotted, and woven in countless ways to make everything from jewelry and tassels to flowers and chandeliers.

This book brings together an eclectic range of attractive and achievable step-by-step projects, all of which incorporate beads in some way. They are easy to follow, whether you are an experienced maker or a novice. There are accessories for the home—a curtain, a cushion cover, or bead-studded fruit. Or why not treat yourself—make a tote bag, a key ring, or a vintage-style corsage. There's plenty of jewelry to choose from, both traditional and cutting edge.

Each chapter covers a particular way of working with beads—wiring, embroidery, threading, and so on—and starts with a comprehensive background section. This shows all the techniques you need to make the projects and gives a few more that, I hope, will inspire you to go on to produce your own individual beaded creations.

Above and right Beautiful contemporary examples of beading design with Murano glass beads, from Ornella Aprosio, Florence, Italy.

part

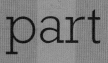

A HISTORY OF BEADING

BEADS IN HISTORY

The story of beads is a fascinating and enthralling thread that runs through the development of trade, social history, and fashion all over the world and links many diverse cultures. The beads that now bedeck our homes, garments, and accessories may appear to be purely decorative, but they have far more significance than as mere ornament.

At various times over the past centuries, beads have circulated across the globe as a trading currency, been used as a means of encoding information, embodied personal wealth, and signposted the social standing of people as diverse as Queen Elizabeth I and the priest-kings of Africa's Yoruba people. They have been threaded, stitched, netted, wired, and woven into jewelry, rosaries, bags, garments, wreaths, and curtains, and any exploration of their background is inextricably linked to the history of manufacture, exploration, and textile arts.

The first beads

The instinct to adorn both ourselves and our surroundings is a very basic one, common to all people, and beads in some form have existed for 40,000 years. The first beads ever strung together were likely improvised from simple materials found in the natural environment: the shells and stones with sea-worn holes we still collect on seaside vacations, or dried berries and seeds that could easily be pierced with basic tools. Thousands of tiny lizard eggs were drilled and threaded by the pre-Columbian people of South America to make necklaces that were prized enough to be buried alongside gold jewelry.

Names

Believed to be the oldest beads so far discovered, a handful of small oval shells with holes drilled through them were found in a Turkish cave. The sea also yields precious gleaming pearls and coral, which are among the earliest materials used to make beads. Indeed, the word "pearl" is interchangeable with "bead" in ancient and modern languages, from Latin and Hindi to French and Italian. Similarly, in Polish and Yiddish, the same name is used for both "bead" and "coral." Jade is represented by the "bead" character in both China and Japan, symbolizing their

intertwined history. (However, the term "bead" itself, derives from the Old English *bede*, meaning "prayer," and has its origins in the rosary beads used for telling prayers.)

Natural materials

As well as found objects, beads were also made from clay and animal by-products such as horn or bone, all local materials which are used to this day. In Soweto, necklaces are made from smoke-fired clay. Animal dung is added to the loaded kiln just before firing, and as it burns, it gives a distinctive soft mottling to the blue-gray beads. Mother-of-pearl from the South Seas, Baltic amber from the coast of Eastern Europe, and Chinese freshwater pearls are all turned into beads. Whitby jet and fossilized Irish bog oak were both prized for their dense black texture, ideal for Victorian mourning jewelry, when etiquette disallowed the wearing of gold or bright gemstones. Trees are also a prolific source of raw materials—beads are made from palm trunks, boxwood, sandalwood, ebony, banana leaves, and palm trunks. Ancient stone beads include agates, Tairona rock crystal from Colombia, and amazonite from Morocco.

Symbols of status

As time and methods progressed, beads began to be made from scarce and precious metals or minerals. Such beads are easily portable and were prized by the nomadic peoples of Africa and Europe: the East African Turkana and the Visigoths alike could wear their wealth and take it with them wherever they traveled. Conspicuous display is always a status symbol—no man or woman could undertake even the simplest physical task while hampered by such jewelry as demanded by high rank and position.

Right A tray of Venetian forate-type glass beads from the mid-twentieth century with intricate lampwork decoration.

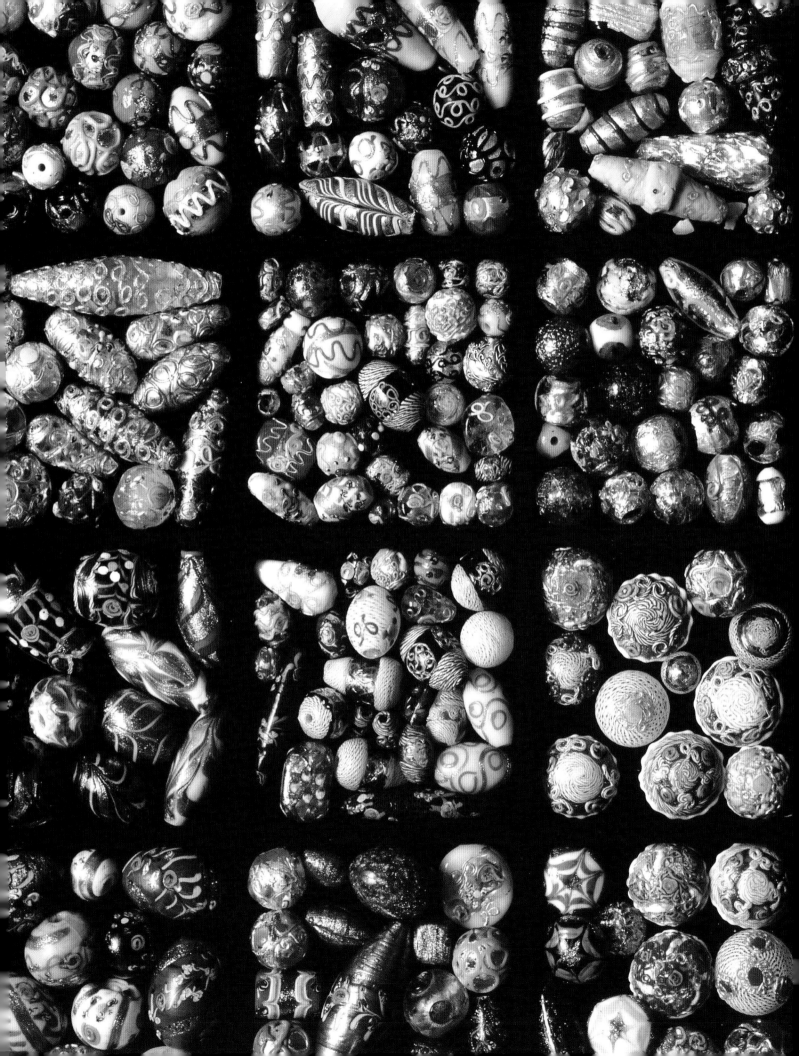

GLASS BEADS

Glass bead makers, or lapidaries, have long been respected for their special skills and the leading practitioners are honored with the title of "bead master." The alchemy involved in producing glass—its fusion of silica (sand) with potash or soda, and the transformation from molten to solid state—still retains an arcane mystery. The actual date when the very first glass beads were manufactured is unknown.

It is variously believed that the first glass beads were either made around five thousand years ago in Mesopotamia or 1,500 BC in Egypt, where faience—a combination of powdered quartz, lime, and copper compound—was used for making opaque, ceramic-like beads. Wherever they originated, the pioneering manufacturing techniques involved were so novel that the beads were valued as highly as gemstones. Bead making has evolved from these humble origins to the highly commercial and mechanized process of today, where holes are drilled by laser and computer-controlled machines are programmed to produce tens of thousands of identical beads.

Wound beads

The simple "wound" beads produced by the ancient Egyptians were made by a method that is little changed today (although the equipment is, of course, far more sophisticated). A plain or colored glass rod is heated in a fierce flame until malleable. The end is then spun around a thick metal wire called a "mandrel," producing characteristic spiraling patterns within the glass. The still-soft base bead may then be rolled in a mold to give it a smooth shape, a process known as "marvering." Any extra glass decoration is added at this stage. The hot beads are left to cool down and harden, or anneal, in a kiln or cooling oven, then the mandrel is removed.

Drawn beads

The second basic method of glass bead making—"drawn" hollow cane beads—evolved thousands of years later as a more efficient process for mass-producing beads. This involves the glass blower creating a hole within the molten glass at the end of the rod and, while it is still hot, pulling the glass out to make a hollow tube. The further the cylinder is pulled, the smaller the beads will be; the tube can be as long as 20 feet. The cooled tube is then cut up into lengths to make small, regular beads that are tumbled in an abrasive powder to smooth off the sharp edges.

Venetian glass

Many of the most beautiful glass beads were—and still are—created by the Italian experts of Murano. The ruling Doges exiled the glass kilns and furnaces from central Venice to this nearby island in 1291. Sent there to avoid the risk of fire spreading through the city, the makers

Below Delicate metal filigree work complements the glass and pearl beads of this Venetian necklace, which was made in 1920.

found themselves confined to Murano because the Doges wished to preserve a monopoly on their flourishing glass industry. The exile lasted until the 1670s, and when the glass blowers did leave, they set up rival centers in Bohemia, Holland, and London.

Of all the Venetian beads, the most intricate are the millefiori glass cane mosaic beads decorated with "a thousand flowers," as the name implies. This technique was invented by the Phoenicians and adopted by the Romans, who used it for bowls and drinking vessels. It was rediscovered in Murano during the early Renaissance (see the bracelet on pages 180–183 for a contemporary take on these classic beads).

Crystal

The first cut-glass crystals evolved in the 1600s. The advent of the grinding wheel, first used on the surface of glass vessels and then on jewels and chandelier drops, meant that multifaceted surfaces could now be created. These sparkled as they reflected the light. Daniel Swarovski, whose descendants are premier in their field today, was the first to develop these machines and he set up production plants in Austria, where he applied the cutting techniques previously used on semiprecious stone and glass.

Trade beads

Glass, ceramic, and stone beads are easily portable and highly coveted—qualities that made them ideal trade goods for dealing with societies where there was no local manufacture. Very early in the history of commerce, beads became a valuable currency that merchants could trade for almost any other commodity. Beads formed worldwide links between distant countries. Trade beads became an essential part of the cargo for Portuguese, British, and other European shipping companies, as important as the iron and copper ingots, which they also carried. Beads were traded for many African staples and luxury items, and before the slave trade was abolished, for male and female slaves.

China had been trading with the rest of the world since the Silk Road opened the doors to the Far East over two thousand years ago. Some of the earliest beads were wound from green glass, in imitation of jade. Others were carved from coral or ivory, or made from cloisonné enamel where a design is formed within a filigree of metal.

Above Strings of beads being used as a trading currency between the Spanish conquistador and Yucatan natives.

Colombus and Cortez carried these first glass trade beads to the Americas. Beads had traditionally been part of ceremonial exchange and trade beads became similarly valued for their novelty and associations with another world, rather than for their monetary worth.

The evocative names of trade beads may reflect their place of manufacture, appearance, or use, but their true origins are sometimes elusive. "Mulberries" and "gooseberries," both popular in Africa, were always thought to resemble their eponymous fruits. Neither "Blue Russians" nor coral-red "Cornaline d'Aleppo" were made in the places whose names they bear, but the latter became known as "Hudson's Bay" beads after the trading company that exported—and still exports beads—to Native Americans. It is recorded that "pony" beads were so called because a hundred of them could be exchanged for a real horse in the early nineteenth century, but other accounts claim the name came about because the traders' only means of transport was a humble pony.

SPIRITUAL POWERS

Beads are an integral part of our daily life and, as such, often go unnoticed. But beads have enormous cultural and religious significance across the globe and there are particular beads, trinkets, and objects made out of beads that have become endowed with special powers and importance.

Particular qualities have long been assigned to various minerals and gems, and superstition dictates that beads made from these stones will transfer their attributes to the wearer. Mothers from Roman times to the Renaissance would adorn their newborn babies with necklaces made from tiny coral beads to bring them good fortune and protect them from the unknown. Turquoise was thought to prevent the wearer from tripping up or falling over, so blue-glazed china or turquoise glass beads are often found as part of the harness trappings for donkeys and camels in Morocco and other parts of North Africa. Amethyst—meaning "not drunk" in Greek—beads protect against intoxication, rose quartz enhances both love and fertility, and jade brings harmony. The recent New Age fashion for spiritual Mala, or power, bracelets made from semiprecious minerals and their glass or plastic imitations continues the tradition. In this instance, the power comes from the wearer who invests the beads with their own aspirations, prompted by the mineral's associations.

Eye beads

Belief in the "evil eye" is widespread and long-established, the idea of its disruptive gaze going back to Neolithic times. By wearing a special charm made in the shape of another eye, many people believe it possible to reflect back and outstare the malign influence, and eye beads, all bearing variations on a motif of concentric circles, are to be found in many countries. Dark turquoise eye beads are now sold as tourist souvenirs in Greek markets alongside strings of worry beads, as are large, flat glass disks with white and yellow schematic eye patterns. These are often hung up over the doorway to deflect the evil eye away from the home. Glass Roman Eye Islamic beads, up to a thousand years old, are still to be found in Mauretania to this very day.

Job's tears

When the kernel is removed from these shiny wild-grass seed cases, natural holes are formed at the top and bottom of the shell, which can then be hardened and whitened in the embers of a wood fire. They are embroidered on to the traditional jackets worn by the Karen people of Thailand to represent the status of married women, but in an interesting comparison, they are also an integral part of mourning ritual in the Highlands of Papua New Guinea.

Below In Papua New Guinea, a widow will smear her body with mud and garland herself with many necklaces made from Job's Tears as a visual expression of bereavement. One strand is then removed every day of the mourning period and the end of the grieving is symbolized by taking off the final necklace and washing away the remaining mud.

Prayer beads

Strings of beads known as "prayer strands" are used as aids to devotion and meditation by followers of diverse faiths, and such revered beads are made from special materials. The Hindu *japamala* consists of 108 beads, often made from the small, round rudraksha nut, which is sometimes known as "tears of God," with a tassel to mark the beginning and end of the prayer sequence. Islam also uses beads and the *tasbih* has thirty-three or ninety-nine beads of wood or date pits from Mecca. Catholic rosaries were once made from rose-petal pulp and new beads should always be blessed by a priest.

Tokens of affection

Gifts of jewelry often embody an intentional extra message. In addition to the qualities of the gemstones, according to a nineteenth-century dictionary of American folklore, a necklace represents unity and continuity, as well as being "a cosmic symbol of ties and bonds." Beaded pincushions and needlebooks, whimsy boxes with embroidered flowers on the lid, each petal a tiny bead, and other small, handmade keepsakes of friendship were frequently exchanged between women. Heavily beaded heart-shaped pincushions brought back from overseas by Victorian sailors were treasured as romantic symbols of love, while in Africa, Zulu and Swazi love tokens were also made from glass beads woven into coded messages and fixed to pins to be worn as brooches.

Africa

The development of beadwork is dependent on the makers having a ready supply of beads, and trade with Europe left a great legacy of beads in Africa, where people had predominantly used seeds, ostrich eggs, and seashells to adorn themselves. Colored beads greatly enriched their vocabulary of pattern and decoration, and a stunning range of decoration can now be found across the continent, some made exclusively for tribal use, some to sell to tourists. The making and wearing of beaded items, each one with its own decorative purpose, is such an integral part of the Masai people's life that their vocabulary contains over forty different terms describing different types of beadwork. Beaded decorations are an important accompaniment to Zulu rites of passage and veils, aprons, or collars are worn as part of marriage ceremonies, pregnancy, and puberty.

Above Many religions use prayer beads or strands as a means of counting when a specific number of prayers is called for.

Wampum

Long before the arrival of glass trade beads, the Iroquois in the South West made their own purple and white beads from hard-shell clams. These were woven into long patterned strips, known as belts, with a message or meaning encoded in the arrangement of the two colors. They were used as an adjunct to ceremony, for reciprocal gift exchange, and in treaty making, but were not used as currency by the people who made them. This usage was adopted by European settlers and explorers who were unwilling to risk taking their own silver or gold coins into unknown territory.

Amulet purses

Women of the Lakota people, part of the Sioux Confederacy, traditionally make beaded pouches to carry their umbilical cords. While pregnant, they will embroider two three-dimensional creatures: a turtle, whose strong carapace has the ability to protect a girl child, and a salamander, whose ability to regenerate a lost tail brings resilience to a boy. When the child is born, the cut cord is folded and placed in the relevant bag, so that the spirit of either animal will accompany him or her throughout the course of their life. The contemporary amulet purses, which often incorporate small charms, fringes, and decorative bead chains, can be seen as a direct continuation of this tradition.

HISTORIC BEADING

Over the centuries, beads have been strung together to make necklaces, bracelets, and belts; woven into strips and panels to sew onto clothing; used to embellish embroidery; or sewn directly on to shoes, bags, and belts. Every imaginable garment or home accessory has been decorated with beads at some stage, somewhere in the world.

Bead embroidery

Beads are a natural adjunct to embroidery, adding texture and color to the basic stitches. Seed pearls, tiny metal spangles, and even beetle wings were incorporated into early ecclesiastical work and garments for the wealthy. The invention of fine, sharp, steep needles in the sixteenth century finally made bead embroidery accessible as a domestic craft. Western bead embroidery became widespread when small, regularly sized beads in a range of colors became commonplace.

Victorians and Edwardians

All beadwork techniques were highly popular during the nineteenth century, lending themselves perfectly to the Victorian passion for decorative surfaces and ornament. Upper- and middle-class women channeled their energy into ladylike pursuits. Craft manuals and step-by-step project books are nothing new: many domestic magazines and publications from this time give detailed instructions on how to make a wildly imaginative array of objects with which to decorate the home. Beads were readily available at this time—small, cork-stoppered vials and tiny canisters of beads could be bought at haberdasheries, where larger quantities were sold by weight, either loose or in prethreaded hanks (hence the term "pound beads").

Bead embroidery on the scale needed for clothing manufacture is a highly labor-intensive process. At this time it was primarily carried out by poorly paid young girls. Fake seed pearls, made from wax-filled glass spheres were very fashionable and complemented the creamy tones of day and evening wear, while at the other end of the color spectrum, dense jet beading encrusted the mourning wear of the bereaved. Beads also featured on boleros, capes, mantles, fringed shawls, and veils, as well as on the parasols that protected delicate complexions from the sun.

American beadwork

At the same time, trinkets made from fancy beadwork became fashionable gifts and keepsakes, particularly in America. Patterns appeared in women's periodicals and were eagerly copied by young ladies anxious to make eyeglasses cases, strawberry-shaped pincushions, book covers, or watch pockets. The distinctive raised and padded technique used small, round glass beads and is characterized by looped fringes and tassels. It represents a fascinating cross-fertilization of cultures, for the stitch is the same as the couched beadwork or lazy stitch of the Native Americans.

Berlin woolwork

Berlin woolwork was the fashionable craze of the 1840s onward, originating in the German city of that name. It was a pictorial form of tent or cross-stitch embroidery. Beads were used to highlight the flat surface of the stitches and some designs were interpreted completely in beads. Glass beads retain their color and do not fade in daylight, so the startlingly bright yellows, reds, and purples that we see now are a reminder of just how intense nineteenth-century color schemes really were.

Historic costume

Elaborate clothing requires decoration, which comes from a combination of richly patterned fabrics and applied surface decoration. Historically, robes for civil and religious ceremony, court dress, and aristocratic clothing have always been sewn with fine silk and metallic threads to emphasize the position and importance of their wearers.

Fortuny

The corseted, rigid Edwardian silhouette gave way to a more natural, comfortable outline, under the influence of the Aesthetic Movement and dress reformers. The most exclusive of these designs came from Italian designer Mariano Fortuny, a true eclectic with a theatrical background. Working from his Venetian Palazzo Orfei in the early 1900s, he viewed his original and innovative garments as works of art. His printed velvets were richly patterned with up to eighteen layers of color and he is best known for his fabulous Delphos dresses, made from undulating pleated silk in a Grecian style. Along with fine silk cords and tassels, these famously featured glass beads, which were specially commissioned from the Murano workshops and used as delicate detailing along the laced seams.

Costume jewelry

In the 1920s, the Western world was looking for an antidote to war and found it in the light-hearted, pared-down fashions of the Jazz Age. Beaded flapper dresses were dressed up with accessories, whereas real jewelry—gold, silver, and precious stones—makes a visual statement about the status and wealth of the wearer, the lighter touch of bold imitation jewelry suited the times. Women who had their own disposable incomes for the first time sought to buy earrings, brooches, or necklaces to accessorize an outfit. Couture houses produced shoe buckles, hair ornaments, and bags decorated with paste jewels and glass beads.

Elsa Schiaparelli, who moved within the Surrealist circle, brought humor to her beaded jewelry, or "bijoux fantasie," designing deep bracelets resembling rose-adorned gold cuffs and a huge "egg" necklace consisting of large, white oval beads threaded onto a black thong. She used beads in realistic trompe l'oeil designs on her fashion designs. Her contemporary Paul Poiret proved that tassels were not just the preserve of soft furnishings, and transformed them into "the tools of coquetry."

Beads in fashion

Style trends change from season to season, veering from minimalism to elaborate ornament. Beads are seldom out of fashion for long, whether in the form of jewelry and other accessories or as an embellishment for clothing. They have long been used to add glamour, sparkle, and a touch

of luxury at all levels, from international haute couture to the popular chains aimed at the teen market. Like magpies, designers scavenge the world for glittering jewels and metamorphose them into something new.

As the decorative emphasis shifts to prints, textures, and patterned fabrics, models invariably appear on the runway wearing beads—as jewelry, sewn onto accessories, or stitched onto garments. British designer John Galliano recently took inspiration from the heavy strands of beads and coins that appear in the traditional, brightly colored dress of Eastern Europe, while the Italian Giorgio Armani, in contrast, is famous for his more muted palette. Working in subtle tone-on-tone, he reinterprets traditional bead embroidery into something undeniably modern.

Accessories complement outfits. The Fendi beaded baguette became the epitome of urban chic, and Chanel's pearls, incorporated into handbag straps, earrings, and trimmings, are instantly recognizable as timeless classics.

Right British designer Alexander McQueen takes beaded accessories to the fashionable limit with this headdress and veil ensemble for the French couture house Givenchy.

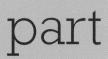

part

2

MATERIALS
AND
EQUIPMENT

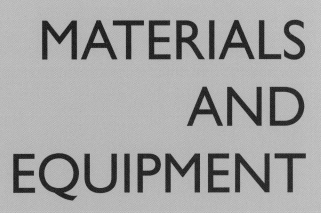

TYPES OF BEADS

Beads come in many different colors, textures, shapes, and sizes. Sourcing the ideal bead for a particular project can be part of the fun: check specialty stores, scour flea markets and garage sales for old jewelry that can be recycled, look for mail-order suppliers listed in books and magazines, or surf the Internet, where a whole world of beads is only a mouse-click away.

Bead sizes are always given in millimeters. Round ones are measured across the diameter. The length of cylindrical or conical beads is usually given, as well as the diameter. The size of the hole may not always be in proportion to the bead, so always check that the thread, elastic, or wire you are using will pass through easily, especially if it will have to go through the bead more than once.

The shape of a bead can be anything from a perfect sphere to a flat disk, and many have special names. Most are variations on a round or oval shape, but there are also cylindrical beads, with either flat or rounded ends and faceted or square sides. Perfectly square beads are called "cubes"; oval, fluted, and melon beads have grooves running along their length; cone beads have a triangular profile; and bicone beads have a diamond-shaped outline.

Glass beads

Some glass beads are individually made, while others are pressed or molded on production lines. The main color comes from the glass itself, whether it is clear, colored, opaque, or transparent. Extra pattern and texture may be created by incorporating metallic foils like the silvery disk in the picture opposite, by using blobs of colored glass within the bead itself, or by adding trails and swirls of molten glass to the surface. The way in which a glass bead is finished will produce a shiny or frosted texture, and various coatings give a pearlized, iridescent, or metallic finish.

Rocailles and bugles

"Rocaille" is a general term for the smallest round glass beads, of which there are at least fifteen different sizes. It is a French word that means "little rock," although these versatile beads actually resemble miniature doughnuts. They are also known as "pound beads" (because they were originally sold by weight), "love beads," or "seed beads." The hole may be round, square, or deliberately off-center, as in Japanese magatama beads. Rocailles are not always completely uniform, so sort through your beads before using them and discard any that are distorted or which have only a tiny hole. If you do incorporate them, any misshapen beads will spoil the finished look, particularly for a woven piece.

"Hex," or "two-cut," beads are short cylinders with six faceted sides. Other small cylindrical beads are sold under various names, including "delicas" and "antiques," and are used particularly for peyote stitch because they have a comparatively larger hole. Bugle beads are longer, from 4 mm to 4 cm, and are cut from fine glass tubes.

Sequins

The original sequins were gold Venetian coins, but now the term is used for any small decorative spangle. Sequins are perfect for creating a sumptuous effect but, with discretion, can make the subtlest of highlights. They are punched from shiny laminated plastic or thin metal. Sequins have a single hole in the center and are either flat or cupped to reflect the light. Larger sequins, known as "pailettes," have more than one hole around the outside edge.

Other materials

Tumbled stone beads are relatively inexpensive to buy and can be mixed with other beads. Black jet and amber have been used since the earliest times. Other natural materials include wood, shells, bone, and, of course, the much-imitated pearl. True pearls will always have a gritty feel when rubbed against the teeth. Even some cheap plastic beads are sophisticated enough for everyday wear.

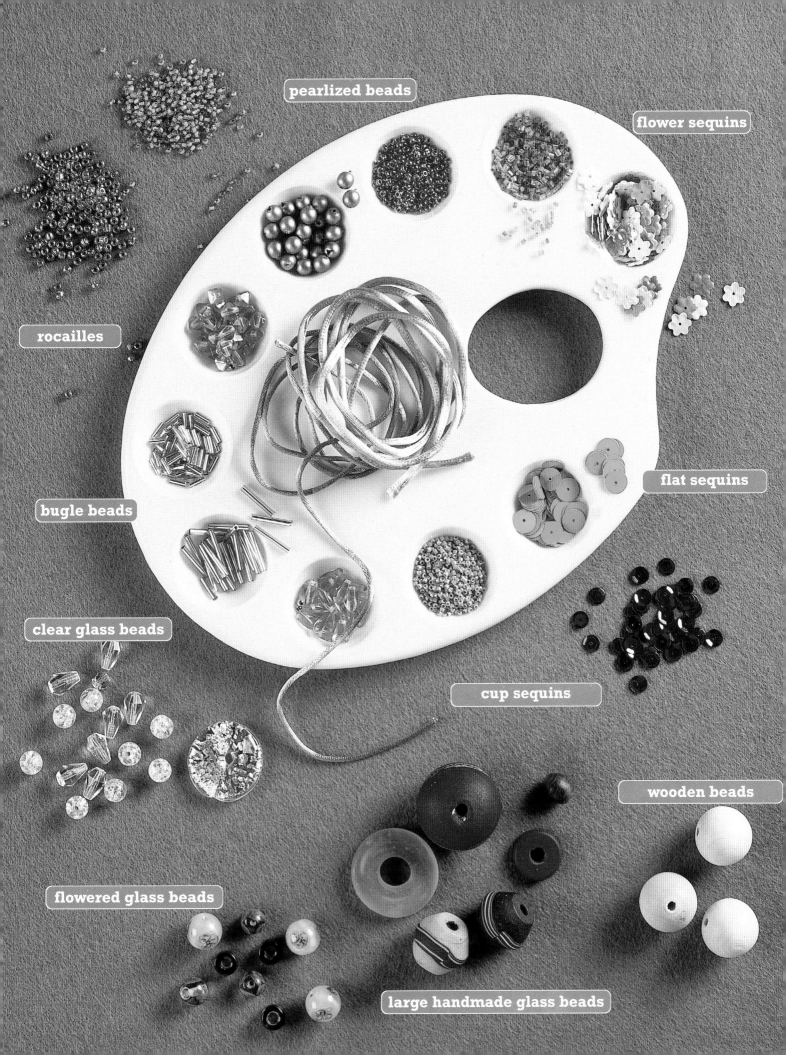

pearlized beads

flower sequins

rocailles

bugle beads

clear glass beads

flowered glass beads

flat sequins

cup sequins

wooden beads

large handmade glass beads

FINDINGS

Fastenings and findings are the clips, pins, loops, and clasps that turn a piece of beadwork into an item of jewelry. Most are made from base metal with a silver- or gold-colored plating, but sterling silver (and even real gold) fittings are also available. Choosing the appropriate size and color of findings can make a handcrafted piece really special.

Fastenings

These all come in two parts to be attached to the ends of a bracelet or necklace. Bolt rings and crab claw fasteners, which are used with a round metal loop, are the most commonly used and come in several sizes. They are spring loaded and do not come undone easily. "Barrels" and "torpedoes" are lightweight and unobtrusive cylindrical screw fastenings, while push snap fasteners may be engraved or studded with diamanté. Loop and toggle fastenings are popular, and many attractive variations can now be found.

Earrings

There are findings to make both screw-on and pierced earrings, but it is advisable to avoid the cheapest versions. Look instead for fittings made from hypoallergenic surgical steel, silver, or gold. Kidney wires and fish hooks (also called ball hooks) loop through the earlobe, but stud or post fittings with a butterfly backing look neater. Earring findings have a small loop for attaching an eye pin or bead.

Calottes

Calottes are designed to give a neat finish to a threaded necklace or bracelet by concealing knots and raw ends and providing a small loop onto which the fastener can be attached. Hinged calotte crimps are used for tigertail and all types of thread: lace-end and leather calottes are for heavier cords and thonging.

Crimp beads

These tiny, ringlike beads come in gold, silver, and black, with a smooth or ridged surface, and they are used for joining ends of thread or monofilament and for spacing beads. The flexible metal is squeezed in place with pliers.

Wire rings

Rings may be circular or oval and come in several sizes and thicknesses. Those used for fastenings are usually soldered for security. The more versatile jump rings are not joined. They are useful for fixing eye pins to earrings or brooch backings, to attach to the top of pendant drops, and to attach fasteners to a finished necklace.

Bead cups and pins

Cups, or caps, are fixed at either end of multistrand necklaces, like the one on pages 40–43, to hide the ends of the many threads in a decorative manner. Thread beads onto eye pins and head pins to make droppers and on to hat pins for a dramatic statement.

Brooch backings

Pin-back brooches can be sewn or glued onto a piece of beadwork. Resembling tiny colanders, these perforated ovals or disks are used to make exuberant, bead-studded brooches. The beads are attached with wire or thread, and the pierced metal part is clipped onto a backing with a pin.

Jump rings or bails?

Jump rings are useful for attaching charms and linking head pins to your work. However, the tapered tops of many drop beads are not suited to jump rings, so three-sided triangular link fittings are used to join them onto earrings or necklaces.

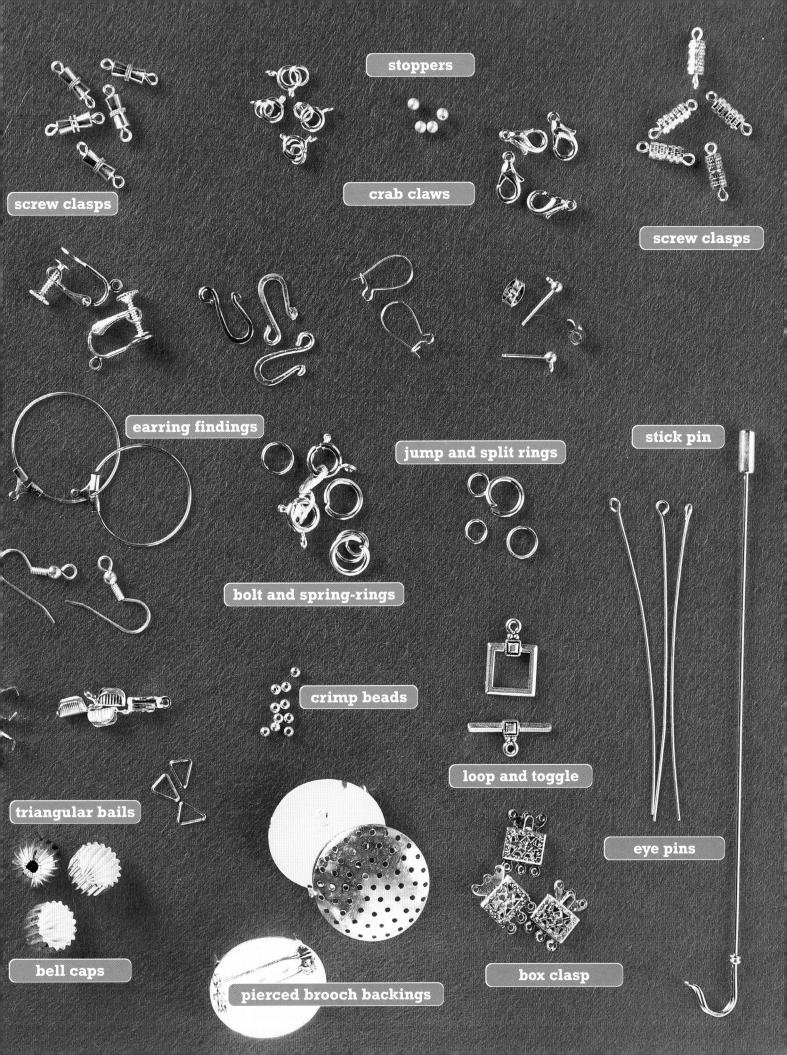

screw clasps

stoppers

crab claws

screw clasps

earring findings

jump and split rings

stick pin

bolt and spring-rings

crimp beads

loop and toggle

triangular bails

eye pins

bell caps

box clasp

pierced brooch backings

THREADS AND CORDS

The color, fiber, and thickness of the thread you use will depend on the size and weight of beads being used: there are several types, each designed for a particular purpose. Threads are graded from the finest, 000, 00, and 0, through B, D, E, and F, to FF, the heaviest, although categories and labeling vary between manufacturers.

Silk cord

This hard-wearing, lustrous cord, made from 100 percent natural fibers, comes in 6-foot lengths on cards with a wire needle or longer lengths on reels. It comes in weights from fine No. 2 to heavy-duty No. 8 for the largest beads, and is always used for knotting pearls or semiprecious stones.

Nylon twist

Twisted polyester thread is cheaper than silk but just as strong. It is good for threading light, smaller beads, but the fibers may stretch in time and fray more easily. Like silk cord, it comes on cards and spools. Bonded nylon undergoes a heat treatment that makes it stronger and reduces the tendency to stretch.

Nymo

An immensely strong yet fine multistranded nylon thread, this comes in many colors and thicknesses, from 000 upward. Choose a shade to blend in with the beads being used, going for the predominant color when several are being incorporated. It is widely used for all weaving techniques.

Monofilament

Like fishing line, this is a strong and flexible thread that comes in black, translucent colors, and clear versions. The finest is just 0.25 mm in diameter and is often used for off-loom weaving. Beads threaded onto it appear to be floating: fix them unobtrusively in place with crimps or blobs of bonding adhesive. Monofilament is not, however, suitable for heavier necklaces, as it may stretch under the weight of the beads.

Elastic

Stretch jewelry cord, which is available in black, white, and several bright, clear colors, is immensely popular for making snap bracelets, chokers, and friendship rings. It is often used with Czech crystals. It comes in three sizes: 0.25 mm, 0.5 mm, and 1.0 mm. Hat elastic and metallic cord are good for threading large beads.

Cords and laces

Round cords range from 1 mm to 5 mm in diameter and are ideal for threading large ceramic, wooden, or pendant beads, and also for children's jewelry. Leather, imitation leather, and cotton laces come in many colors, as does flat suede lace and thong. Less attractively, but more descriptively, satin cord is also called "rat-tail," which is a shiny, soft, round cord that comes in a range of colors and thicknesses, from 1 mm to 3 mm.

Ribbon

Fine polyester and narrow silk ribbons are good for threading pretty beads and can be knotted like silk cord if necessary. The ribbon becomes a feature of the finished piece.

Tip

When threading Nymo, flatten the cut end between your finger and thumb so that it will pass easily through the eye of the needle. Buy all the beads and threads you will need for a particular project at the outset, along with a few spares. You may not be able to match them at a later stage, and however careful you are, a few beads will always manage to escape.

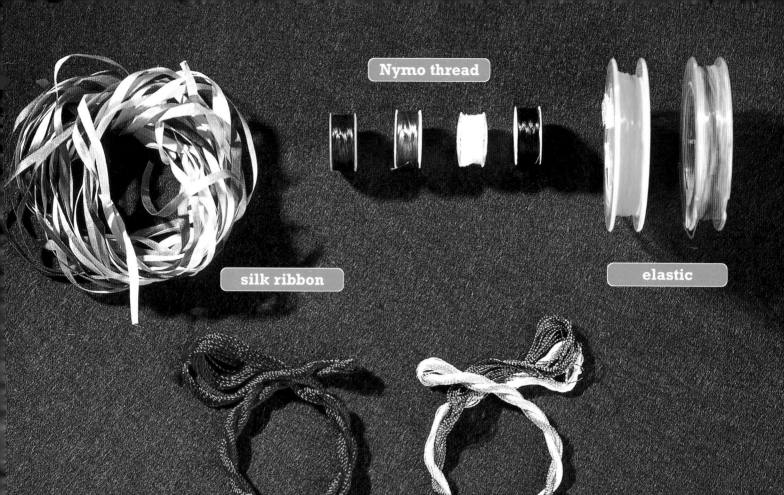

Nymo thread

silk ribbon

elastic

embroidery threads

satin cord

suede lace

WIRE

Wire is made from a variety of metals, from pure silver or brass to alloys such as nickel. The malleability, or flexibility, of the wire varies—head pins require a rigid length of relatively strong wire, while wrapping needs a fine wire, which bends easily. The thickness or diameter of all types of wire is given as the gauge, which ranges from 10 to 40 plus the letter "g."

Wire gauge

The smaller the gauge, the heavier the wire, so 10 g is the thickest and 40 g is the thinnest. These measurements are industry standard, but for comparison and to make choosing the wire you need for a particular project easier, the chart gives the equivalent metric and standard (U.S.) measurements. Fine 24 g wire is flexible enough for making beaded flowers and wrapping techniques, while heavier 20 g is good for making earrings or other jewelry that needs to be sturdy.

gauge	inches	mm	gauge	inches	mm
10	0.1019	2.59	26	0.0159	0.404
11	0.907	2.30	27	0.0142	0.361
12	0.0808	2.05	28	0.0126	0.321
13	0.072	1.83	29	0.0113	0.287
14	0.0641	1.63	30	0.01	0.254
15	0.0571	1.45	31	0.0089	0.226
16	0.0508	1.29	32	0.008	0.203
17	0.0453	1.15	33	0.0071	0.179
18	0.0403	1.02	34	0.0063	0.160
19	0.0359	0.912	35	0.0056	0.142
20	0.032	0.813	36	0.005	0.127
21	0.0285	0.724	37	0.0045	0.114
22	0.0253	0.643	38	0.004	0.102
23	0.0226	0.574	39	0.0035	0.089
24	0.0201	0.511	40	0.0031	0.079
25	0.0179	0.455			

Metal wire

Gold wire is expensive and the preserve of jewelers, but gold-plated wire or craft wire in a gold finish is available. Pure silver wire tends to become dull after a while, but nickel wire is a good and cheap imitation. Brass tarnishes, but can be polished, and copper wire is very flexible and relatively inexpensive.

New manufacturing techniques mean that the range of colored wires is constantly expanding to include beautiful shiny finishes, from pinks and reds to greens and yellows. The basic wire is a copper alloy and the colored coating is permanent. Available in various gauges, these are ideal for projects where the wire is visible: choose a shade to complement the beads.

Tigertail

This stringing wire is made from tightly twisted strands, like a miniature steel cable, and coated with a layer of clear or colored nylon. It comes in a range of metallic colors and thicknesses from 24 g to 30 g, and can be used for both heavy and sharp-edged beads—see the lariat on pages 44–47 for a good use of the finest gauge. It is not possible to straighten out any kinks, so it should be stored and used with care.

Memory and spaghetti wire

A heavy wire that will "remember" its shape when cut into lengths, memory wire comes in coils of three diameters: ¾ inch for making rings, 2 inches for bracelets, and 3¾ inches for choker-type necklaces. Use heavy-duty cutters and pliers when working with this industrial-strength metal.

Spaghetti wire is a fun new idea: these springy, hollow coils can be looped into bracelets or cut into lengths and used as spacers between beads. The colors are bright and young, and they are a favorite with children.

covered wire

brass wire

spaghetti wire

fine gauge wire

memory wire

copper wire

colored craft wire

TOOLS

As with any craft, it is important to have the right tools for the job before you begin any beading project. However, not all types of beadwork require lots of equipment, and some of it you may already have: off-loom weaving, for example, requires only a needle and thread. Start off with the minimum and invest in wire-cutters, pliers, or a loom as your interest progresses.

Pliers

Ideally you should have three pairs of pliers, each with a distinct purpose: round-nose, for making neat round loops; either snipe-nose pliers or fine angled pliers, which have a flat inner surface and a rounded outer edge for opening jump rings and squeezing crimps; and flat-nose pliers for holding work in progress and closing crimps and triangles. If you buy only one pair, snipe-nose pliers will perform most tasks adequately; domestic pliers are too clumsy, and their ridged jaws will mark the wire. For the real enthusiast, crimp pliers are specially designed with two sets of notches for attaching crimp beads, and pliers with plastic-coated jaws help to protect soft metal.

Wire-cutters

Wire-cutters, an essential part of the kit of any beader or jewelry maker, are used for snipping wire and tigertail. (Don't be tempted to cut tigertail with scissors— it is tougher than it looks!)

Scissors

Narrow-bladed, sharp embroidery scissors are useful for snipping threads and trimming knots, and curved manicure scissors are good for the finest work. Cutting-out scissors for sewing projects should be kept for fabric only, as paper will blunt the blades.

Needles and pins

Needles are graded from a heavy-duty size 1, up to the very finest, size 16. Size 10 embroidery needles, which have a flat eye, are useful for stitching rocailles and bugles, and for off-loom weaving techniques using sewing cotton or Nymo thread. Quilting needles, also called "sharps," have round eyes, which are better for threading monofilament. Bigger beads require a thicker needle, size 8 or larger. An assorted package of embroidery needles will cover most tasks. Check that the needle will pass through the bead you are sewing, and if it will have to go through more than once, always choose a smaller size. Blunt-ended tapestry needles are useful for threading large beads. Slender beading needles are used for loom-weaving; they are long enough to pass through all the beads on the weft. They have a long eye for easy threading but tend to snap or bend under the least pressure, so keep spares nearby.

For pin-beading techniques, use special short pins, which are half the usual length. These are available from good craft suppliers and fabric stores.

Needle threaders

These are good for threading narrow ribbon, Nymo thread, or stranded floss through the eye of a needle, but not for the tiniest needles, as the wire loop will not fit through small eyes.

Thread conditioner

Wax has traditionally been used to strengthen sewing and beading threads, but it can build up and clog the needle after a while. New silicon thread conditioners coat the fibers with a fine layer of silicon, which prevents tangling and knotting. This is helpful, because you can work with longer threads and, consequently, use fewer knots.

Glue and nail polish

A small bit of bonding adhesive will secure knots at the ends of necklaces and bracelets and on woven items. Choose a tube with a fine nozzle for accurate application. Clear nail polish can be used for the same purpose and also for stiffening thread so that it can go through beads without a needle.

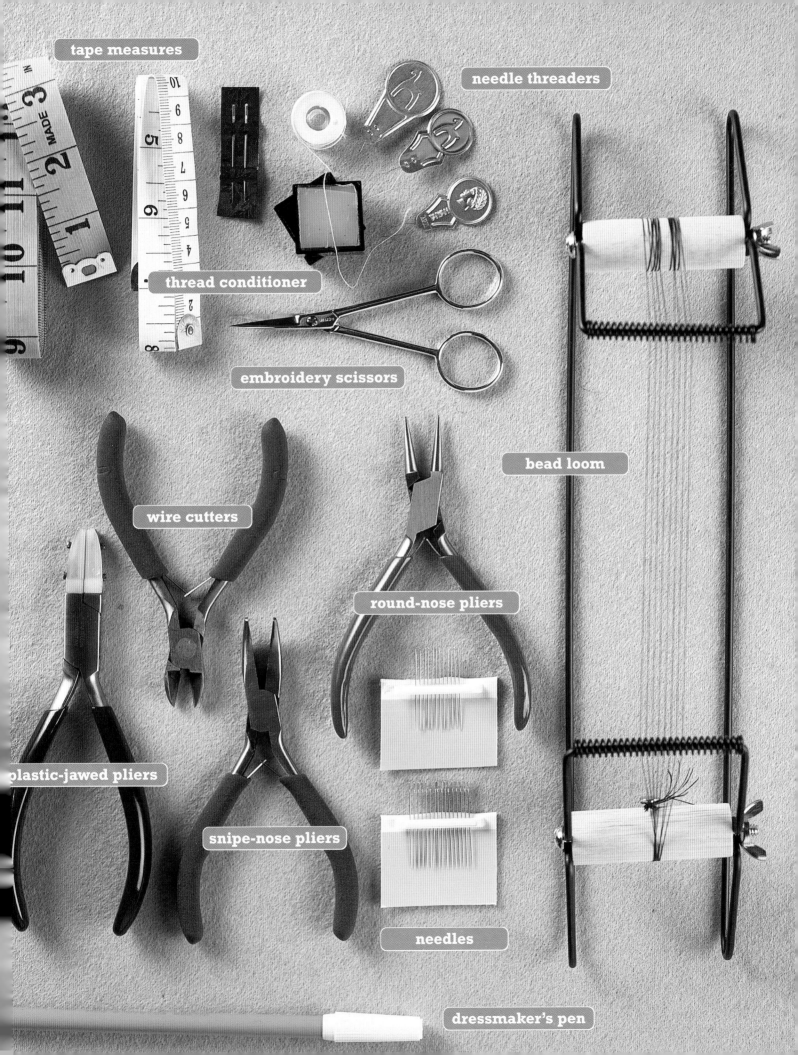

part 3

TECHNIQUES
AND
PROJECTS

THREADING

Depending on the look you wish to create, threaded necklaces and bracelets can be classic, funky, or formal. They can be made up of beads that are matching, clashing, carefully graduated, or selected randomly. String them together in long, short, single, or multiple strands, and wear them with panache.

Bead management

Rocaille beads and bugle beads are usually bought by weight; small amounts come in cylinders with plug lids, while larger amounts are sold in prestrung bunches. This is useful because a needle and thread can be passed alongside the cotton to rethread them without having to undo the loops.

Loose beads are often packed into small resealable plastic bags, but since these do not always remain closed, it is a good idea to move them into more secure containers. Once any beads, particularly the smallest, have been removed from their original packaging, they have an inevitable and irritating tendency to roll away. A necklace-planning tray, which has U-shaped grooves and a flock finish, is useful for sorting and arranging larger beads, while smaller rocailles and bugles can be kept in shallow saucers or little trays lined with velvet or thick cotton fabric. Pick up one bead at a time with the point of the needle, or slide them individually onto the end of thicker threads. A traditional—and easier—method of threading seed beads is to tip them into a bowl and repeatedly pass a beading needle or the end of a wire through them with a rhythmic, scooping motion. Each pass will capture several beads.

Threading beads

A bead can be threaded onto anything that will pass through it, from string, twisted silk, or a sturdy leather thong to wire or even a safety pin. For some projects, the thread is an integral part of the finished design and as important as the beads, but for others it is purely utilitarian. Always choose a thread that is strong enough to support the weight of the beads and flexible enough for its purpose and which will go easily through the hole without being damaged.

Tip

Fine threads require a fine needle—size 10 or a special beading needle—while monofilament, cord, or elastic can simply be pushed through the bead. A coating of nail varnish will strengthen the cut end, and silicon thread conditioner or wax will help prevent the thread from tangling and fraying.

Making a necklace

Necklaces vary from 16 to 44 inches, and there are evocative traditional names for the standard lengths: from the shortest to the longest, dog collar, princess, matinee, opera, and Charleston were all originally designed to suit a specific neckline.

When cutting the thread for any necklace, always allow at least 12 inches of extra thread for ease of working. Make a slipknot 5 inches from one end to prevent the beads

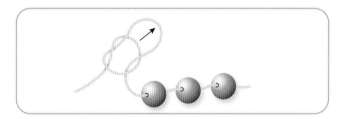

from slipping off. This should then be undone before knotting the ends or attaching the fastener.

Joining the ends

When making an elasticized bracelet or a necklace of 30 inches or more (that slips over the head without needing any fastening), the ends of the thread are knotted together with a reef knot or joined with a crimp or both (see page 34). Join on an extra length of thread when weaving beads with a reef knot, trim the ends, and secure with clear glue.

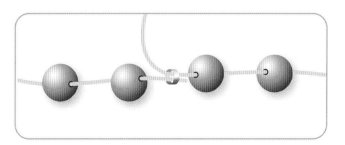

Tying a reef knot

Also known as a "flat knot," this is a very secure knot that will not slip. The knot is made in two steps: follow the diagram and remember that Girl Scouts once learned how to do this by repeating "right over left and under; left over right and under."

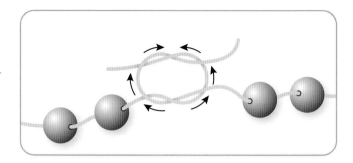

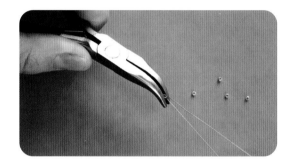

Joining with a crimp

Pass the two ends of the thread to be joined through a crimp bead and pull them up tight. Maintaining this tension with one hand, squeeze the crimp with pliers to fix it in place firmly. Trim the ends to ¼ inch, and glue them down if preferred.

Spacing beads

Adding extra space between beads is a good way to emphasize their decorative qualities, and it also makes just a few beads extend to a bracelet or even a necklace.

Spaghetti wire is a recent innovation that does this job very effectively: simply snip the fine coil into equal or random lengths with wire-cutters, and thread them alternately with the beads.

Knotted strands

Semiprecious gemstones and pearls are traditionally strung with a small knot in between each bead. This prevents any erosion caused by them rubbing against each other and, if the necklace is broken, keeps them all from rolling away. Special silk twist, which comes threaded onto its own fine wire needle, is a good choice for heavier beads. It is available in an attractive range of colors and several thicknesses.

Make an overhand knot close to the last bead and insert the point of a thick needle through the open loop. Use the point to guide the knot along the thread until it lies against the hole. Maintaining tension with the needle, gently pull the other end of the thread to tighten the knot.

Cords and thongs

Handmade and one-off beads can be threaded onto a shiny rat-tail cord or leather thong, which then becomes as visually important as the bead itself. Make a simple choker by knotting either side of a large bead, or for a flat bead with a central hole, as pictured here, fold the cord in half, pass the loop through the bead, and pull the two ends up through the loop to form a "lark's knot."

Double-strand threading

Buttons and beads make natural partners: use near-invisible monofilament to make them appear as if they are hanging without support. Cut a piece 2½ times the finished length, and fold it in half. Slide a button to the midpoint, then pass the ends back through the second hole. Thread them both through a bead, then through both holes of a second button, one from front to back and the other from back to front. Continue to the end.

Take one end from front to back through the holes in the next button, and the other end from back to front. Thread a button head one length through a bead, then from back to front through two holes in a button. Repeat this for the required length, then take a second thread from front to back through the last button, through the next bead, and so on to the end.

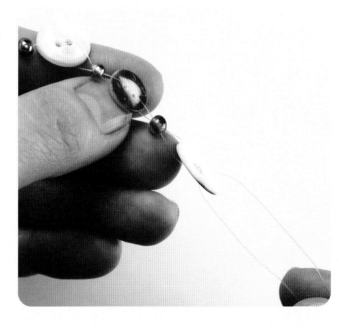

Multistrand threading

Several bead strands of the same length can be joined together at the ends for an informal look, as with the multistrand necklace on pages 40–43, but there are some designs in which each separate row must lie flat and be seen individually. Spacers and separator bars are used for this. The spacer is a decorative finding with a loop for the fastener on one side and two or more loops on the other: mount a thread on each of these. Keep the strands apart by threading on separator bars at intervals, and finish off with a second spacer. For a bracelet or choker, the strands should be the same length, but for a necklace, each one should be progressively longer.

Threading on elastic

Elastic is ideal for threading bracelets of one, two, or more strands. It comes in different colors and thicknesses, and the variations are endless. Thread the elastic through the finest possible needle, then add at least 7 inches—the average wrist measurement—of beads. For this simple interlacing, thread a feature bead followed by rocailles and bugles in a repeating pattern. Thread the elastic back through the big bead, repeat the first length of small beads, and then go through the next rocaille. Repeat to the end and finish off with a crimp or a reef knot and glue (see pages 34–35).

Threading on safety pins

Safety-pin bracelets are widely made by women's collectives in South Africa, where innovative bead crafts go back many generations. You will need an even number of pins; about 74 will fit around an average wrist. Thread large-holed beads along the spike, and then fasten the pin. Join the pins together with two rounds of elastic. Thread through the top of the first, then the bottom of the second, and so on, alternating the direction but keeping all the beads facing outward. Pass the second round through the remaining holes. Fasten the elastic with crimps or knots and glue (see pages 34–35).

Where to find other threading techniques

Knotting double strands
Collector's necklace: pages 168–171

Threading on monofilament
Floating necklace: pages 48–51

Multistrand threading
Multistrand necklace: pages 40–43

Threading on ribbon
Gift bags: pages 114–117

Spacing flowers and beads
Bead curtain: pages 184–187

Threading on tigertail
Choker and bracelet: pages 52–55

Spacing with crimps
Lariat: pages 44–47

Threading onto head pins
Chandelier: pages 56–59

Light Pull

This is a really simple project that shows off these unique glass beads to their best advantage— as well as making the light pull easier to find in the mornings.

1 Slip one end of the thong through the ring and fold back the bottom 1 inch. Bend the last ⅓ inch of the wire at right angles and place this short end halfway down the loop. Coil the long end of the wire several times around the thong, using pliers as necessary to pull it tightly, then clip the ends of both thong and wire.

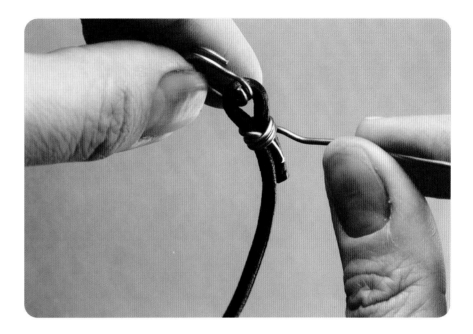

2 Use the pliers to make a small loop at one end of the remaining wire, then thread on the beads. Clip the loose end to ½ inch. Bend this into a loop, slip it over the split ring, and secure with the pliers.

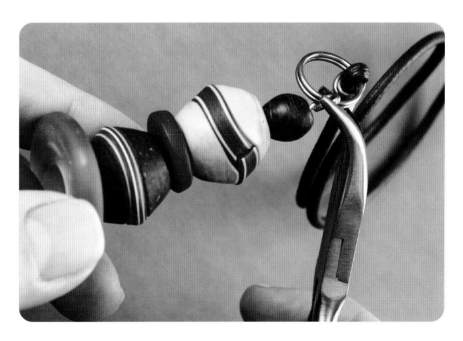

YOU WILL NEED:

- 3 feet of thick leather thong
- small copper split ring
- 6 inches of soft copper wire
- round-nose pliers
- wire-cutters
- approx. 6 large handmade glass beads

Multistrand necklace

There are twelve strands to this colorful necklace, here in shades of blue and green—choose any shades of beads and vary the tones and textures, as well as the patterns. The finished necklace measures approximately 19 inches; add extra beads to each strand for a longer version.

YOU WILL NEED:

- tape measure
- 32 feet polyester thread
- scissors
- fine beading needle
- 10 grams each of 12 types of beads in different colors, varying from 2-mm rocailles to 4.5-mm bugle beads
- round-nose pliers
- 2 silver eye pins
- clear glue
- ⅓-inch-diameter silver bell caps
- 2 silver ⅓-inch round beads
- wire-cutters
- silver fastener and jump rings

1 Cut a 30-inch length of polyester thread. Thread on the first rocaille bead approximately 6 inches from the end, and pass the needle through the hole once again, securing it on the thread. Add on an additional 18 inches of beads in the same color. Pass the needle twice through the final bead to lock them in place.

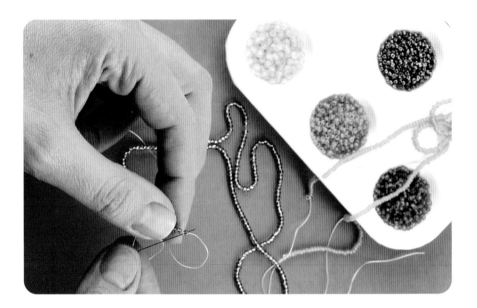

2 Make another eleven strands, each using a single color, and one strand of alternating rocailles and bugle beads.

3 Lay all the strands side by side on a flat surface, lining up the beads exactly. Pick up all of the threads, then tie them together with an overhand knot. Use the pliers to pull the ends through and to slide the knot down toward the beads. Make a second knot just above the first.

4 Open up one of the eye pins with the pliers and slip the hook over the threads, in between the knots. Close the loop again, squeezing it tightly with the pliers. Make two or three more knots so that the pin is fixed securely to the threads. Put a dab of glue on the knots, allow to dry, and then clip the ends. Thread a silver bell cap and a silver bead on to the pin.

5 Use the wire-cutters to trim the eye pin down to ⅓ inch. Bend the wire into a tight curve with the pliers, slip on a jump ring, and close it into a loop.

6 Finish off the other end of the necklace in the same way and attach the fastener to the eye-pin loops. Twist the strands of the necklace gently together before wearing to create the characteristic ropelike appearance.

Lariat

The name for this necklace comes from the Spanish word for lasso, *la reata*. The ends are not joined up, but rather they are tied together—or in this case, threaded through one of the loops— to create an attractive, free-hanging double pendant.

YOU WILL NEED:

- 27 inches of fine (0.31-mm) tigertail
- 28 silver crimp beads

for the pendants:
- 2 x 12-mm round beads
- 2 x 10-mm crystal beads
- 2 x 8-mm round beads
- 2 x 6-mm rondelles

for the main part of the lariat:
- 5 x 4-mm oval crystal beads in each of 6 colors
- 5 x 4-mm bicone crystal beads in each of 7 colors
- 10 grams of 2-mm rocaille beads in mixed colors
- flat-nose pliers
- wire-cutters

1 Start by folding the tigertail in half and slide a crimp bead down to the center. Squeeze it flat with the pliers. Squeeze the crimp bead gently, as they have a tendency to snap and break—have some spare ones on hand just in case. Flat or needle-nose pliers are best for this operation.

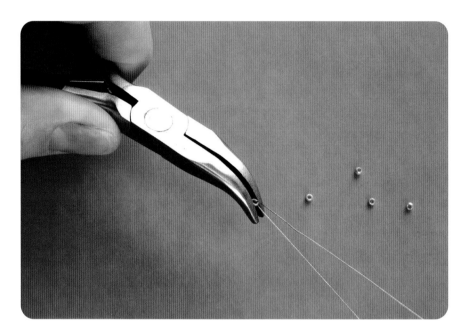

2 To make the pendant end, thread both ends of the tigertail through the first four beads: a 12-mm round bead, a 10-mm crystal bead, an 8-mm round bead, and a 6-mm rondelle bead. Hold them in place with a crimp.

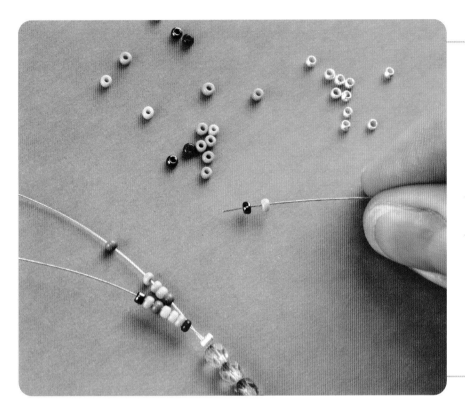

3 For the main part of the lariat, thread five matching bicone beads and another crimp. Thread three rocaille beads onto one end of the tigertail and two onto the other. Fix a crimp bead over both strands ¾ inch along from the last crimp. Add five oval crystal beads, and secure these with a crimp, close to the last bead. To make the loop, thread 15 rocailles onto each strand and secure with a crimp over both strands of tigertail.

4 Add 5 more bicone beads, then continue threading alternating blocks of oval beads and bicone beads, with 5 rocailles on the two strands between them, until the lariat measures 23 inches. Leave the last crimp unsqueezed.

Finish off with a second pendant to match the first, then thread on a crimp. Pass both strands of tigertail back up through the pendant and the first five crystals. Gently pull up the ends so that there is no slack, and squeeze the two crimps to secure. Clip the ends with wire-cutters.

Floating necklace

This delicate necklace is made with the finest monofilament, which is almost invisible, so that the three strands of beads appear to be floating in midair. The finished necklace measures approximately 17 inches; allow extra monofilament and beads for a longer version.

YOU WILL NEED:

- 3 yards fine monofilament
- scissors
- approximately 70 beads in shades from clear crystal to dark purple
- 2 silver clamshell calottes
- silver crab-claw clasp
- clear adhesive glue
- snipe-nose pliers
- 2 silver jump rings

1 Cut a 24-inch length of monofilament. Thread a bead 2 inches from one end, then take the leading end back through the bead and pull the resulting loop up tightly to secure the bead. Continue adding more beads at irregular intervals of ¾ inch–1½ inches, until the beaded length measures 15 inches. Trim the remaining monofilament to 2 inches.

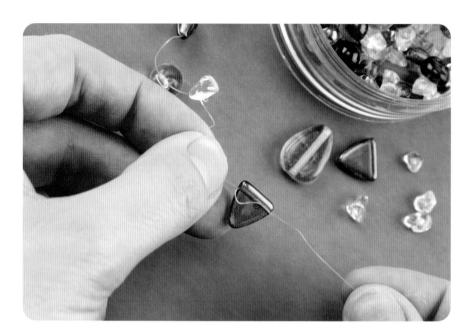

2 Make another three strings of beads in the same way, and lay them side by side on a flat surface. Thread the four loose ends at the left through a clamshell calotte (see pages 22–23).

3 Knot the ends together, using the pliers to pull the knot up tightly. Put a small dab of clear glue on the knot, leave it to dry, and then trim the ends closely. Squeeze the calotte gently with the pliers to close it and conceal the knot. Do the same at the other end.

4 Fix a jump ring on to the clasp, then bend the loop of one calotte around the jump ring, using the pliers. Fasten the second jump ring to the other calotte (see page 61).

Choker and bracelet

Crimping is a versatile technique that, once grasped, will give you plenty of new ideas. Some of the rocaille beads used here are transparent with a colored center so that the color radiates through with the light.

YOU WILL NEED:

- 80 inches of colored tigertail
- wire-cutters
- 18 crimp beads
- snipe-nose pliers
- 2 large and 2 small clamshell calottes
- 10 grams of 2-mm rocaille beads in 3 different colors and finishes
- 1 large and 1 small jump ring and clasp
- 1-inch length of chain

Both the choker and bracelet are tight-fitting: check neck and wrist measurements before starting and, if necessary, adjust the tigertail measurements accordingly.

1   Cut three lengths of tigertail: 14, 15, and 16 inches long. Hold them together in one hand and line up the ends. Thread a crimp bead over all three strands, then squeeze it tightly, very close to the ends, using snipe-nose pliers. Slip the loose ends through a calotte, and squeeze it shut, concealing the crimp.

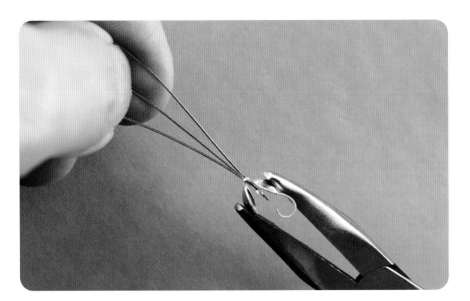

2   Fix a crimp onto each strand, 4 inches from the calotte. Thread 5 inches of the first-color beads on the shortest strand, then secure them with a crimp. Put 6 inches of the second-color beads on the center strand and add a crimp, then thread and fix 7 inches of the third color on the longest strand.

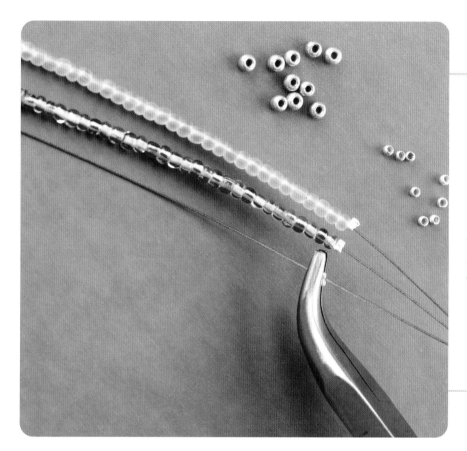

3 Thread another calotte over the three threads, then join the loose ends together with a crimp. Close the calotte over the ends, and add on the clasp and jump ring fastener.

4 Fix the chain to the jump ring. Make the bracelet in the same way from three 7-inch lengths of tigertail, each threaded with 4 inches of beads, beginning 1 inch from the end of the wire.

Chandelier

This project recycles the metal parts of a paper lantern shade. Any stripped-down frame can be used, depending on the effect desired. The type and shape of beads used is an individual choice because the chandelier is a unique design.

YOU WILL NEED:

- long head pins
- a selection of glass and plastic crystals, faceted beads, long bugles, and chandelier drops
- wire-cutters
- round-nose pliers
- scissors
- monofilament
- wire lampshade frame
- bonding adhesive

Allow 1 large crystal drop and between 3 and 7 round crystals per strand.

1 The pendants at the end of the long bead drops are made on head pins. Thread on three or more crystals, and trim the remaining wire to ⅓ inch with wire-cutters. Using the tip of the round-nose pliers, bend the top of the wire into a small loop (see page 62).

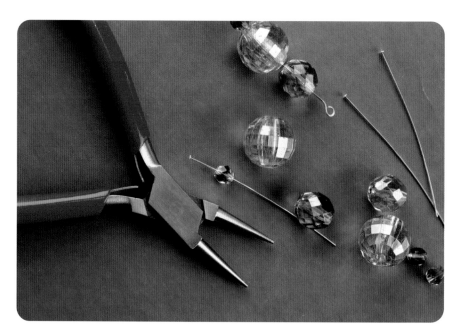

2 Cut a 10-inch length of monofilament, pass it through the wire loop, and secure the pendant by tying a reef knot in the center. Additional beads should then be added by threading them onto both ends of this thread.

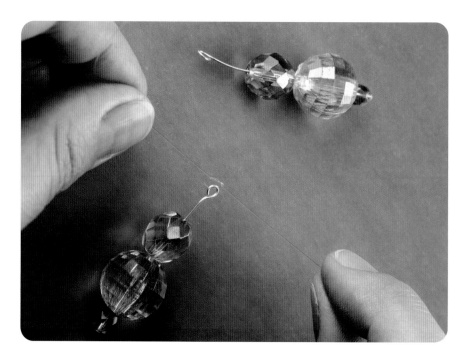

3 Prepare the chandelier drops by carefully removing the original hanging pin; use pliers and, if necessary, wire-cutters to do this. Thread a 10-inch length of monofilament through the top hole, and knot in place. Add on one or more crystal beads. Add the remaining crystals and beads to the drops, varying the lengths, colors, shapes, and amounts used for each one.

4 Tie on the drops by wrapping the monofilament three times around the wire frame and securing the end with two overhand knots over the top of the strand. Clip the end and reinforce the knot with a bit of bonding adhesive. It is important to balance the weight of the drops evenly as they are fixed so that the finished chandelier will hang properly. Do this by slipping the frame over a tall, heavy object and adding the drops, one at a time, from alternating sides.

FASTENINGS & FINDINGS

Some findings are as important as the beads themselves and form part of the basic design: pearls and diamanté-studded clasps sit decoratively at the back of the neck, while loop and toggle fastenings are often worn at the front.

Calottes

Before the fastening is joined on, a calotte is usually fixed onto each end of the thread. These small, hinged spheres contain and conceal the raw end, acting as a link between the necklace and the clasp. They have a loop at one side and a hole for the thread at the other; the way in which they are attached varies according to the type of thread. Three different methods are used in this book: calotte with bead—Daisy Necklace, step 4, page 137; calotte with knot—Choker and Bracelet, step 1, page 54; calotte with crimp—Floating Necklace, steps 3–4, page 51.

Gimp and knots

❶ Gimp—a fine wire tube—is used to reinforce silk twist or other delicate thread where it passes through a fastening. Finish the necklace with a ⅓-inch length (omitting the knots between the last two beads if the necklace is knotted), then pass the needle back through the final bead.

❷ Leaving a small space between the second and third beads from the end, make a half-hitch knot over the thread, then pass the needle through the second bead along and make another knot. Slide the needle through the next bead and clip the remaining thread, securing with a tiny dab of clear glue. Attach the other end of the fastening in the same way, having left the first two beads unknotted.

Leather calottes

Also called a lace-end calotte, this wraps around the end of a leather thong or length of thick cord and is squeezed firmly in place with pliers. Fit a jump ring or fastening through the hole.

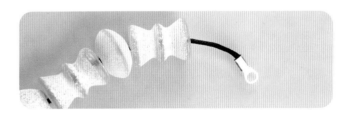

Barrel screws

Hollow barrel or torpedo fasteners are made in two parts that screw together. Thread one part onto each end of the necklace, and tie one or two overhand knots at the end of the thread. Use a needle to slide these down inside the hollow and trim the thread, finishing off with clear glue.

Jump rings

Round jump rings have many uses, including attaching fastenings to calottes and eye pins to earring findings. Soft metal rings can be opened gently by hand while heavier ones require two pairs of flat-nosed pliers. Rather than prying the two sides apart, which will cause distortion, twist one side forward and the other backward. Slip the finding loops onto the open ring. Holding one side firmly with the pliers, close the ring by using your finger and thumb or a second pair of pliers to twist the other side backward. A tiny bit of superglue will secure the ring completely.

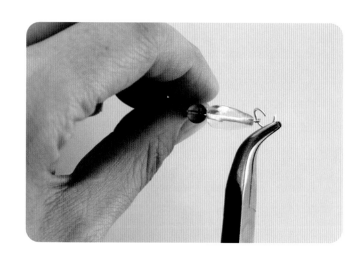

Using wire pins

Wire pins—lengths of thick wire with a stopper at one end—are used for making earrings, charms, and pendants. There are two types, eye pins and head pins, which come in different gauges and lengths, in gold or silver finish.

Eye pins

Widely used for making earrings, they finish off with a small loop that is used for attaching drop beads or, as pictured here, clusters of small pendants. Use pliers to twist one side of the loop forward to open it up, thread on the pendants, and twist it back to close.

Head pins

These end with a round stopper, like the head of a dressmaker's pin. If the bead slips over this, first thread on a small rocaille to keep it in place.

Making a loop to finish off

After threading on the beads, clip the end to approximately ⅓ inch. Grasp it firmly in a pair of round-nose pliers, about halfway down, depending on the size of the loop required. Gently roll the pliers backward, while holding the wire firmly against them, to form a circle. When it is almost complete, bend the wire forward at the point where the loop ends to form a question-mark shape. This action centers the loop above the pin. Move the pin down to the tip of the pliers and bend it around to close the loop.

Attaching earring findings

Slip the open loop onto the small loop of a ball hook or post stud fitting before closing. Be sure to have the earring finding facing the right way if your earring has a right and a wrong side. Stud findings are attached in the same way and should come with a butterfly backing attached.

Angled eye pins

If the eye pin ends with a drop bead or a charm, remember to make the top loop at a right angle to the bottom loop, so that the finial will face forward when the pin is mounted onto another finding.

Triangular links

Like the bails on pages 22–23, these are used to fix drop beads or other pendants onto eye pins and jump rings. Ease the two sides apart with pliers, position one on either side of the hole, and gently squeeze them together.

Barrette findings

Hair-clip findings are pierced with holes at either end. Use these to anchor a length of wire threaded with large beads or to secure the end of a length of thread. Add on beads and single silk blossoms, wrapping the thread around the bar as you go. Work back in the other direction to fill in any spaces with additional beads and flowers.

Vintage Earrings

This is a chance to reuse those old broken necklaces from the bottom of your jewelry box and give them a new lease on life. Here, semiprecious beads are combined with shiny new findings to give them a new feel, while maintaining that fashionable vintage look.

YOU WILL NEED:

- selection of old beads or broken necklaces
- new beads to match
- wire-cutters
- 2 silver bails
- 2 short silver eye pins
- 30 short silver head pins
- round-nose pliers
- pair of silver earring fittings

Allow 1 large crystal drop, and approximately 30 other small beads for each earring.

1 Carefully dismantle the jewelry, using pliers to cut the old wire. Wash the beads in warm soapy water and leave on some paper towels to dry.

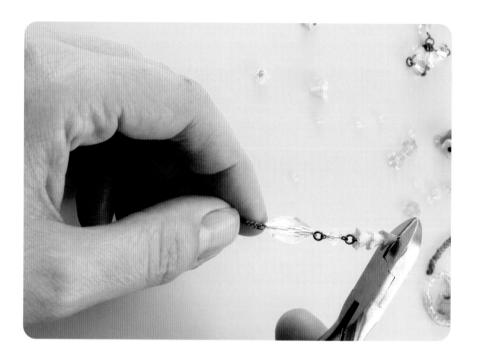

2 Choose a long drop bead to form the lower part of the earring and fix a triangular bail through the hole. Fix the loop of the eye pin through the bail.

3 Make fifteen droppers from a mixture of old and new beads, varying the length from ¼ to ½ inch. For each one, thread two or more beads onto a head pin, trim the end to ¼ inch, and bend the wire into a tight loop with the pliers.

4 Thread the droppers onto the eye pin, starting with the longest and positioning them carefully to form a cluster. Finish off with two small beads. Bend the end of the wire into a tight loop, and attach it to the earring fitting.

Charm Bracelet

A simple chain is transformed into a bracelet that combines beautiful glass beads with silver charms. Head pins and jump rings are used to link it all together. Silver is used here to complement the blue beads, but gold or brightly colored metals could be used just as easily.

YOU WILL NEED:

- 2-mm silver beads
- 1-inch silver head pins
- selection of silver and glass beads
- wire-cutters
- round-nose pliers
- silver jump rings
- silver chain-link bracelet
- a few silver charms

Allow 1 jump ring, 1 large glass bead, and a selection of small beads for each link on the bracelet.

1   If the hole through the first decorative bead is wider than the head, start by threading a silver bead onto the head pin to act as a stopper. Add on two or three more beads. Trim the end of the wire if necessary, so that there is approximately ¼ inch free, then bend it into a loop using round-nose pliers (see page 62).

2   Open up a jump ring by gently easing it apart with a sideways twist (see page 62). Slip one end through the wire loop. Fix the dropper onto the bracelet by slotting the jump ring onto the second chain link, then close it with pliers.

3 Continue making and adding charms, varying the shapes and colors of the beads, until the bracelet is complete. You will need to make one dropper for every link or for each alternate link if the chain is fine.

4 Finish off by adding the silver charms at regular intervals, fixing them next to the droppers with jump rings.

Brooch

This exciting and modern brooch is inspired by a sea anemone—the arms are short and spiky with pretty sequin flowers. If the tendrils were longer, they would hang down softly, giving the brooch a whole new look, so experiment depending on the final effect desired.

YOU WILL NEED:

- scissors
- 4-inch square of silky fabric
- 1-inch brooch back
- air-erasable pen
- size 10 embroidery needle
- matching sewing thread
- 5 grams each of light blue, assorted translucent, and opaque white ¼-inch bugles
- 5 grams of apricot, pinky red, and clear rocailles
- 5 grams of turquoise ⅝-inch bugle beads
- flower-shaped sequins
- pair of pliers

1 Cut a 2-inch-diameter circle of silky fabric. Run a gathering stitch around the circumference. Place the perforated disk centrally on top. Pull up the gathers, enclosing the disk. Fasten the thread securely. Divide the disk into three sections with an air-erasable pen.

2 Thread the needle with a double length of thread. Knot the ends together, and bring to the right side through a hole in one section. Thread on two light blue bugle beads and an apricot rocaille bead. Slide the beads down the thread, and insert the needle back through the bugle beads. Pull the thread taut so the beads stand upright. Continue applying beads in this section with lengths of two, three, and four light blue bugle beads and single turquoise bugle beads.

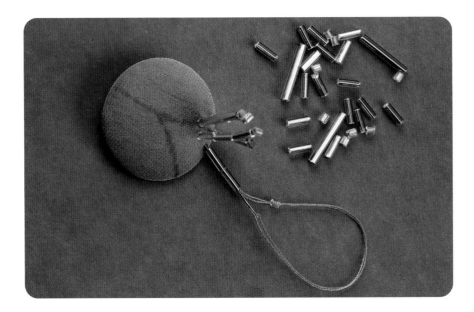

3 Move on to the next section and thread on three assorted translucent bugle beads, a sequin, and a pinky red bead. Fix the beads as before by inserting the needle back through the sequin and bugle beads. Continue applying similar beads in this section with lengths of one, two, and three translucent bugle beads and sequins.

4 Move on to the last section and fill with lengths of one and two opaque white bugle beads and clear beads, as before, by inserting the needle back through the sequins and bugle beads.

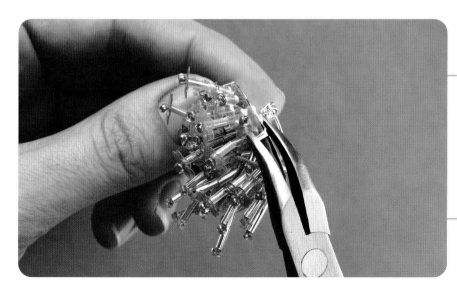

5 Place the disk on the brooch back. Bend the prongs over the disk with a pair of pliers to secure in place.

WIRE BEADING

Wire brings another dimension to beading, giving it a more solid and sculptural form. Traditionally it has been used to create flowers, leaves, and petals for ornate glass posies, or even to make dolls' furniture. More recently, technological developments such as tigertail and memory wire have broadened the scope of bead jewelry-making.

Wired beads

Beads mounted on individual wires can be joined together or interspersed with a length of chain to make a delicate necklace. Bend one end of the wire into a loop and thread on a bead (see page 62). Clip the wire, leaving an end of ⅓ inch, and twist it over to form a second loop. Ensure that both loops lie in the same direction. Wire the next bead in the same way, slipping the first bead onto the bottom loop before closing.

Memory wire

This hardened steel wire comes in preformed coils of three different diameters, which are specifically designed to make rings, bracelets, or necklaces. Use heavy-duty cutters to snip it into separate loops or spirals of two or more rounds—it will retain its curved shape and cannot easily be bent. Almost any bead can be threaded onto memory wire, but tiny delicas, which have comparatively large holes, are especially good for rings. A round of these can be alternated with a length of spaghetti wire for an interesting effect.

❶ Memory-wire jewelry does not need fasteners. To start and to finish off, twist the end of the wire into the smallest loop possible, using round-nose pliers (and a bit of effort, since the wire is very tough).

❷ As an alternative, using bonding adhesive, glue special stopper beads, which are drilled only part of the way through, onto the cut ends. For extra strength, you should also stick the two adjacent beads to the wire.

Wire binding

It is not easy to drill holes in polished pebbles and smooth nuggets of sea glass, but by binding them with a wire cage, found objects can be turned into pendants or earrings.

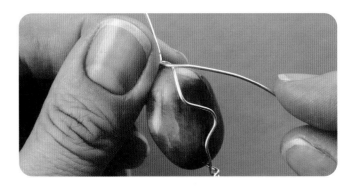

❶ For a 1-inch stone, cut a 10-inch length of medium-gauge wire. Leaving a 2-inch length at the top, wrap the long end around the front and back of the pebble, twisting it into a small loop at the bottom. Bending the wire into a series of curves will add to the decorative effect and increase the coverage. Twist the working end around the "stalk" and back down the right side.

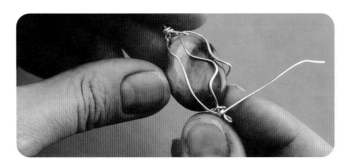

❷ Wrap the wire around the bottom loop and back up the left side, adding more curves as you work. Finish off by bending the stalk down into a loop and wrapping the working end tightly around it. Clip with wire-cutters, and use pliers to turn under any sharp ends.

Wrapping

For this deceptively simple technique, thread beads onto fine, flexible wire, and coil it around a headband, bangle, or, more ambitiously, a wire lampshade frame. Wrapping works best when the beads are of a single size and shape—rocailles are ideal. Thread on all the beads you will need and start off by wrapping the wire a few times around the surface to be covered, coiling it back over the cut end to secure it. Slide the beads down, and begin wrapping the wire over and under the foundation.

To cover a lampshade, first bind the top and bottom rings with a continuous round of beads. Fix a length of wire to the top of each vertical strut and secure a long bead-threaded wire to the top ring. Wrap the beaded wire around the frame. To keep it in place and prevent it from sagging, twist the loose wires over the beads and back around the heavy wire each time it passes over a strut.

Here the wire has been used to wrap around a headband for a special occasion. Small gold beads are threaded onto the wire all at once. First secure the wire at one end of the headband, then wrap the wire around, using the teeth of the headband to keep the coils regular, and then bind it at the other end.

Tigertail

Strong, nylon-coated tigertail has a springy quality that makes it the perfect foundation for interlaced beading. This Victorian-inspired jet choker incorporates black crimps to secure the coiled wire unobtrusively. Thread on a crimp, followed by a rocaille, a faceted bead, a rocaille, and another crimp: these will lie along the top edge. Add a faceted bead, seven beads to hang at the bottom of the loop, and another faceted bead, and then thread the long end of the tigertail back through the crimps and the first three beads. Pull up into a circle and squeeze the crimps tightly. Thread on a long bugle bead, then repeat the process, always threading the wire through the first large bead on the previous loop before passing it through the top beads.

Where to find other wire beading techniques

Crocheting with wire
Napkin rings: pages 164–167

Threading beads on heavy wire
Light pull: pages 38–39; Crystal hearts: pages 80–83

Threading beads on tigertail
Lariat: pages 44–47; Choker and bracelet: pages 52–55

INTERMEDIATE

Crystal hearts

These translucent hearts can hang in a window or at the top of a sheer curtain and will bring a little shabby chic to any home.

YOU WILL NEED:

- 3¼ feet of medium-gauge silver wire
- wire-cutters
- round-nose pliers
- selection of crystal and clear glass beads in various sizes
- 12 inches of fine monofilament

Allow 50 assorted clear glass beads and drop beads for each heart.

1 To make the dropper, cut a 2-inch length of silver wire, and bend one end into a small loop with the round-nose pliers. Thread on a pear-shaped bead and a colored crystal, trim the other end to ¼ inch, and bend it into a loop.

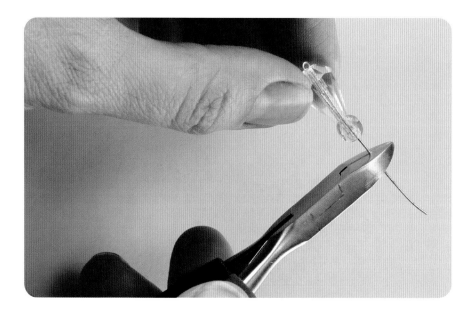

2 Cut a 30-inch length of wire and fold it in half. Thread on the dropper so that it sits on the angle, then thread on approximately 7 inches of small beads, followed by one large bead. Add another 1½ inches of beads, then bend the loose end of the wire around to the left. Wrap the end between two beads, 2½ inches from the dropper. Trim the end to ¼ inch, and secure it around the foundation wire with the tip of the pliers.

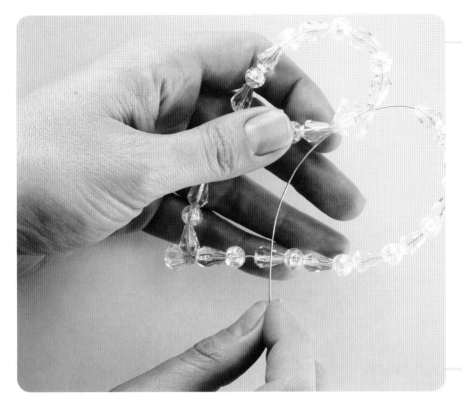

3 Thread another 7 inches of beads onto the other end of the wire, ensuring that the two sides are symmetrical. Pass the loose end down through the large bead, then add another 1½ inches of beads and finish off the right side as for the left.

4 Make a small loop in the top of the remaining wire, and thread through the monofilament. Tie the two ends together to make a hanging loop. Push the other end of the wire through the center of the large bead and thread on more beads until they reach the tip of the heart. Clip the end of the wire to ¼ inch, bend it into a loop with the pliers, and secure it over the wire, next to the dropper.

ADVANCED

Blossom

This beaded stem is truly an exotic and rarified plant. Created from pearlized beads, make your own in any color and height that complements your vase or make a whole bouquet to fill your home.

YOU WILL NEED:

- 15-mm silver-plated wire
- wire cutters
- round-nose pliers
- 100 x 6-mm pearlized glass beads
- reel of fine colored wire
- 20 x 10-mm pearlized glass beads
- at least 60 assorted 4-mm beads in same color palette

1   Cut a 15-inch length of silver-plated wire. Using round-nose pliers, bend one end into a small loop.

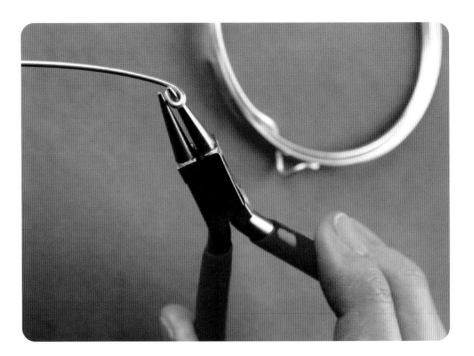

2   Thread three 6-mm beads about a quarter of the way along a 12-inch piece of colored wire and twist the ends together to create a stem.

3 Continue twisting until the stem measures about 1½ inches, then thread on another three assorted smaller beads. Leave a space of ½ inch and twist the two ends together to make another blossom.

4 Add on 2 medium-sized beads and then twist the ends of the remaining colored wire along the thicker wire, close to the loop.

5 Repeat this process, varying the number and color of the beads in each blossom until the top part of the stem is full. Link each fine wire stem onto the top loop to keep it from sliding downward.

6 Continue until you have a large and luscious bloom or run out of beads, then twist any remaining wire down the stem.

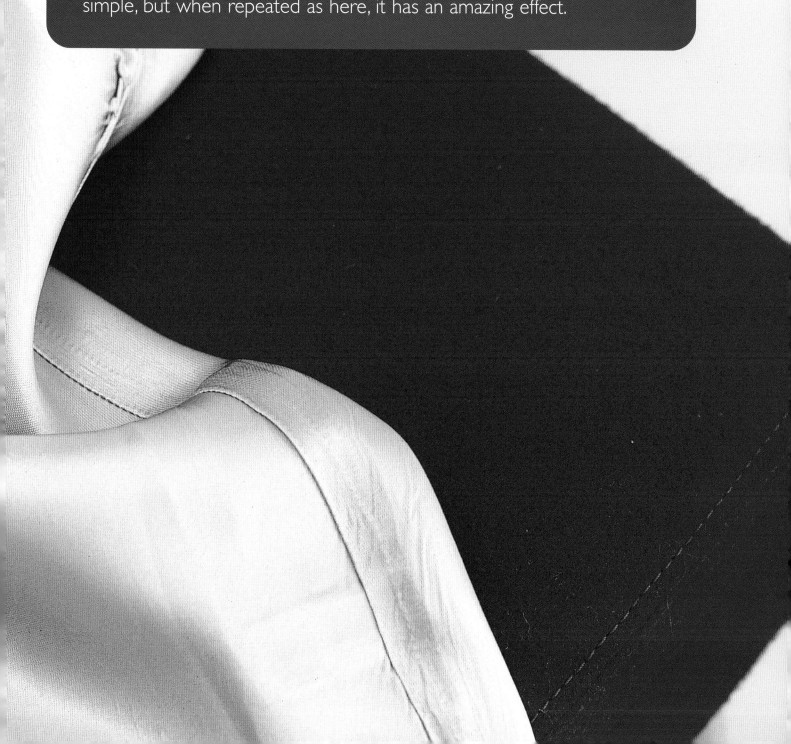

Lilac Corsage

This beautiful flowered corsage would make a fantastic addition to any outfit. The flowers are made with a French wire technique, which is simple, but when repeated as here, it has an amazing effect.

YOU WILL NEED:

- 1-ounce container each of 3 shades of blue and lilac satin-finish two-cut hex beads
- 102 x 2-mm silver-lined gold rocaille beads
- reel of 0.6-mm pink craft wire
- wire-cutters
- 4 x 14-inch No. 22 paper-covered wire
- florist's tape
- 6 velvet leaves
- 1-inch-diameter perforated disk brooch backing
- matching sewing thread
- sewing needle
- flat-nose pliers

1   For each pair of flowers, thread at least 120 rocaille beads onto the reel of wire. Thread on three gold beads, and twist them together about 3 inches from the end of the wire to form the flower center.

2   Slide down the next 15 beads and make them into a petal by twisting the wire twice, close to the flower center. Make the second petal in the same way.

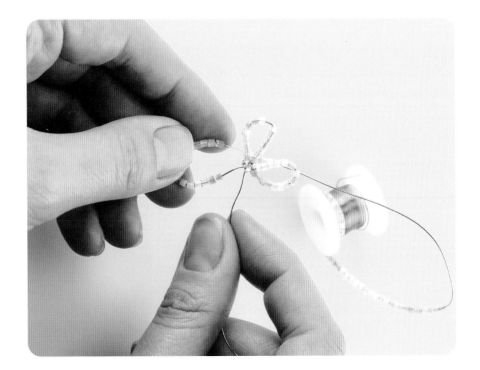

3 Make another 2 petals, then twist the 2 loose ends together twice to form a flower. Clip the wire 3 inches from the petals. Be careful not to twist the wire too tightly or it will break.

4 Thread ten beads onto each loose wire. Cut a 2-inch length of paper-covered wire for the stem, and twist the ends of the pink wire tightly around it.

5   Make a second flower and attach it to the other end of the stem. Bind the stem with florist's tape, wrapping it tightly at an angle over the wire.

6   Make another 16 double stems in the same way, varying the length of the wire from ⅔ inch to 3 inches. Shape the flowers by twisting the straight ends together and gently easing the four petals into shape, bending them up and back to form a realistic flower head. Bend each wire in half.

7 Clip the wire stalks from the velvet leaves, then stitch them around the outside edge of the pierced brooch front, using a double length of matching sewing thread.

8 Sew the flowers securely onto the brooch, again using a matching thread. Start at the center with the tallest stems, then work outward. Fix the brooch backing in place with flat-nose pliers. Gently ease the leaves and flowers into a pleasing arrangement by bending the wires into the desired position.

EMBROIDERY

Beads and sequins can be used to enhance and embellish embroidery stitches to highlight areas of a patterned fabric or can be used on their own to create intricate designs and generally to add texture, color, and sparkle. Fringes and tassels (pages 110–117) are the perfect accompaniment to bead embroidery, providing a stylish finish for bags, cushion covers, or lampshades.

Getting started

Any fabric is suitable for embroidery, provided that it is strong enough to support the beads you have chosen. Fine silk and organzas can be backed with a layer of lawn or calico to give them extra weight, if necessary, although bead embroidery on sheer fabrics can look stunning. Ideally, the fabric should be mounted in an embroidery hoop or tapestry frame to keep an even tension across the work and prevent the stitches from puckering. Always sew beads with the finest possible needle: the size of holes often varies in a batch of rocaille beads, but tiny delica beads have uniformly larger holes in comparison to their size. Take care when sewing down bugle beads, as the cut edges are sharp and may damage the thread.

Sewing cotton or any type of embroidery thread can be used for beadwork: choose a color to match either the beads or the background color, whichever looks the least intrusive, and choose a weight suited to the size of the beads and the texture of the fabric.

Sewing single beads

To sew on a single bead, bring up the needle, thread on a bead, and then take the needle down one bead's width away from the starting point. Make the bead extra secure by working another stitch through the hole. Small rocailles and seed beads can be scattered across a surface or sewn together more densely for a more solid look, while longer bugles look effective stitched side by side to form a solid line, or end to end to make a zigzag.

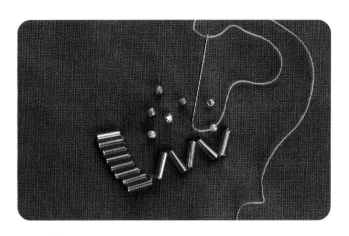

Satin stitch

This stitch is similar in appearance to bead weaving, and by using more than one color in a row, you could create interesting geometric patterns. Bring the needle up at the bottom corner, then thread on up to five small beads (any more and the loops become too long). Lay them across the fabric and take the needle down at the end of the row. Work a second stitch through them for security, then continue sewing short rows of beads in the same way, spacing each new stitch a bead's width apart.

Couching

Bead couching is useful for curved outlines and swirly lettering. Start by lightly drawing the shape onto the background fabric with a pencil line or dressmaker's pen. Bring the needle up at the start, and thread on approximately 2 inches of beads. Lay them along the marked line, and take the needle down again. Bring a second thread up on the line, just below the first bead, and make a small stitch across the first thread, tying it to the fabric. Repeat this couching stitch to the end of the line, ensuring that each bead sits neatly on the line. Here, the top part of the letter has already been worked, and the second row of beads is being couched down from the bottom left corner. To make a smooth join in a longer line, bring the needle up through the final bead of the previous row, and then thread on more beads.

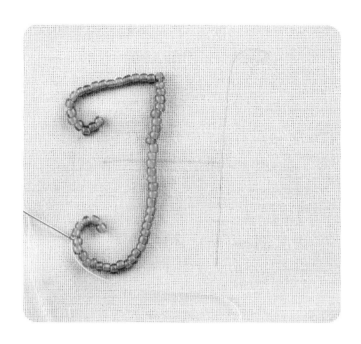

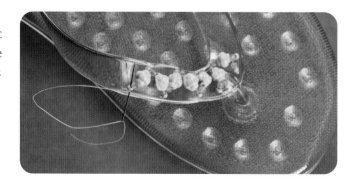

Counted beadwork

Counted beadwork, or beaded tent stitch, is often used to give added emphasis to cross-stitch designs but can also be used on its own to work monograms, numbers, and simple patterns. When following a chart, one colored square represents a single bead. All the beads lie diagonally in the same direction. Use a counted thread fabric for the background: for aida, work one stitch over each block, and for finer fabrics sew one bead over a block of two or more threads. Here, each bead is sewn over a square of two threads in each direction. Bring the needle out at the top left, thread on a bead, and take the needle down two threads across and two threads down to the bottom right.

Sewing on other surfaces

There is no need to restrict embroidery to the usual fabric backgrounds: beads can be sewn onto anything that can be pierced by a needle, so be inventive when looking for items to decorate. This simple plastic flip-flop is transformed into a fashionable piece of footwear with the addition of just a few toning beads. To make sure that the beadwork will be hard-wearing, a strong nylon thread has been used, and the knots have been reinforced with clear glue.

Sequins

Sequins have always had an inherent glamour—think of sparkling 1950s cocktail dresses, evening bags, and glittering dancing shoes. Used on their own or in conjunction with beadwork and embroidery, sequins are perfect for creating a sumptuous effect but, with discretion, can make the subtlest of highlights. They are punched from shiny laminated plastic or thin metal and come in many different colors and shapes—stars, flowers, hearts, and diamonds. Small round sequins have a single hole in the center and are either flat, or cupped to reflect the light. Larger sequins, known as paillettes, have more than one hole around the outside edge.

Sequins and beads

The most decorative way to sew on a sequin is by securing it with a small bead in a matching or contrasting color. Bring up the needle, thread on the sequin followed by the bead, and then go back down through the hole. As usual, work a second stitch to reinforce the first, then bring the needle up a short distance away for the next sequin. Sew a bead in each hole of a pailette.

Overlapping sequins

Flat sequins can be sewn down singly with a stitch from the hole to the outside edge, but look best when the thread is concealed. Do this by working them in overlapping rows, like fish scales. Bring up the needle and thread on the first sequin. Take the thread down close to the edge, then come up again a sequin's width from the starting point. Thread on another sequin, and take the needle down at the edge of the first one. Continue in this way, making back stitches to the end of the line.

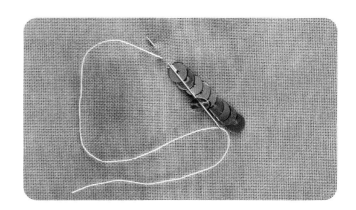

Embroidery tip

If you are sewing a large quantity of small beads, it can prove time-consuming to keep returning the needle to a saucer or lid full of beads. To make life easier, roll out a small circle of reusable putty adhesive, and press it into the beads. Keep this on the surface of the fabric, close to the embroidery, and pick up one bead at a time on the point of your needle.

Beads and Buttons Bag

This cute bag is just right for using up all those odds and ends at the bottom of the sewing basket. Created here in blue linen from a tablecloth and old checkered shirt fabrics, it has a vintage charm.

YOU WILL NEED:

- scissors
- 3-inch x 10-inch strip of white linen
- 14-inch x 20-inch piece of blue linen
- 20-inch x 11-inch piece of blue shirting
- dressmaker's pins
- tacking thread
- sewing machine (optional)
- matching sewing thread
- 4-inch square of fusible webbing
- small scraps of shirting
- iron
- pinking shears
- selection of 35 old buttons
- 1 gram mixture of rocaille beads to match
- air-erasable pen
- fine beading needle

from blue linen cut:
front: 8-inch x 10-inch rectangle
back: 10-inch x 11-inch rectangle
handles: 3-inch x 20-inch strip
from the shirting cut:
lining: two 10-inch x 11-inch rectangles

1 Pin and tack the strip of white linen to the bottom edge of the blue bag front. Sew together ¼ inch from the edge, then press the seam flat. Draw nine leaf shapes, from 1 to 2 inches long, onto the fusible webbing, and cut out roughly. Following the manufacturer's instructions, iron onto the shirting, and cut out with pinking shears. Peel off the backing papers and iron into position on the bag front.

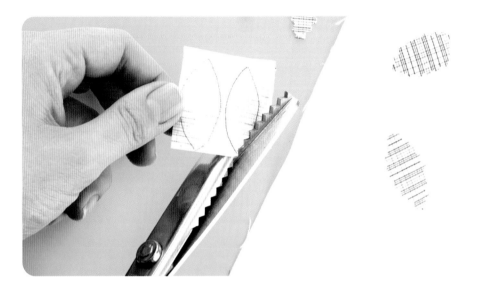

2 Arrange the buttons to form two tall flowers, sprinkling a few others across the bottom for a border. Mark the positions with an air-erasable pen, then place the buttons on a sheet of paper in the same positions. Sew them on, either with matching thread or by sewing rocaille beads through the holes. Add more rocaille beads in rings around the round buttons.

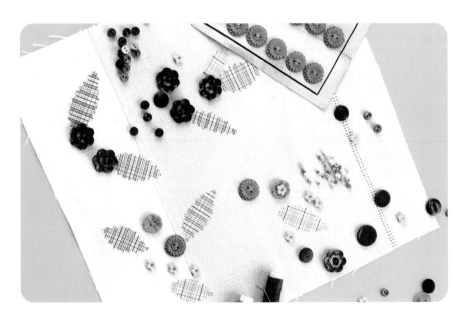

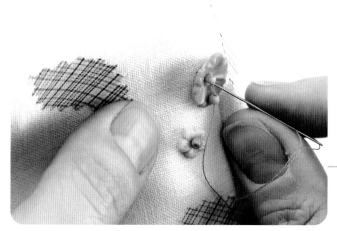

3 Place the back panel over the right side of the completed front panel. Pin and tack around the side and bottom edges, then sew together, leaving a ¼-inch seam allowance. Clip the corners and turn right-side out. Press the seams gently. Fold and tack under ¼ inch, turning around the open edge.

4 Pin and tack the two lining pieces together along the side and bottom edges. Sew together, ¼ inch from the edge. Clip the corners and press all the seams to the wrong side. Tack and press over ¼ inch, turning around the top edge.

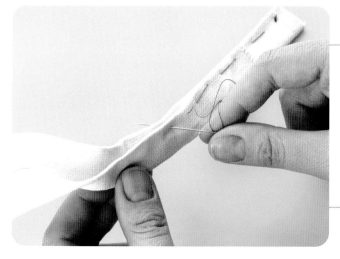

5 Press the handle strip in half lengthwise. Turn each raw edge to the crease and press in place. Refold the strip along the center crease, and tack the folded edges together. Top stitch ⅛ inch from each side edge, then cut the strip in half.

6 Pin the handles inside the top edge of the bag, 1 inch from the corners. Slip the lining inside the bag. Line up the seams, then pin and tack the two top edges together. Top stitch ⅛ inch from the edge to finish.

Brocade Cushion Cover

The simple idea of outlining the pattern on the material here has a dramatic effect. The complementary colors of lime silk brocade and burgundy organza heighten the theater. Use up any fragments that you have, the more luxurious the better.

YOU WILL NEED:

- tape measure
- scissors
- remnants of plain silk, lining fabric, organza, and patterned brocade in toning colors
- pins
- sewing machine
- tracing paper
- fine pen
- colored pencil crayon
- matching sewing threads
- 10 grams each of rocaille and bugle beads in two main colors to match
- approx. 20 matching sequins
- rectangular cushion pad

1 For the front panel, cut six strips of silk, each ½ inch longer than the depth of the pad and of varying widths, allowing for a 1-inch seam on each strip; their total width should be 6 inches wider than the pad. Cut one broad strip of brocade as a central feature and add a plain strip of silk to each side. Pin and tack the strips together, then machine stitch ⅓ inch from the edge. Press the seams open. Trim the panel to the same size as the pad.

2 Pick out a motif from the main brocade and trace its outline from the remaining fabric. Cut out around the pencil line, and pin the paper template onto the fabric. Using a pencil crayon, draw the missing outlines onto the adjacent strips.

3 Using a color to match the fabric, sew a line of closely spaced single rocailles around the edge of the main motif, stitching them along the pencil outline where necessary. Outline the inner shape of the motif in the same way.

4 Pick out a few details by using the bugle beads in a contrasting color to emphasize the patterns featured on the fabric.

5 Add a few larger and contrasting beads and one or two sequins as highlights in the shapes.

6 For the back, cut a rectangle of organza the same depth and 2 inches narrower than the front panel. Cut a 5-inch-wide strip to the same depth. Sew a narrow double hem along one short edge of the main piece and one side of the strip. Matching the raw edges and right sides, lay the main piece across the front, and pin the top, bottom, and side. Do the same with the strip. Tack and machine stitch ⅓ inch from the edge, clip the corners, and turn through. Press lightly, then insert the cushion pad.

Appliqué Blooms

These flowers don't need to be restricted to flip-flops. Attach them to your jeans, a jacket lapel, or your favorite summer bag. The silk dupion here lends a bright shimmer, but these blooms would also look great in striped cotton or a colorful felt for the colder seasons.

YOU WILL NEED:

- 2 x 5-inch squares of silk dupion
- 5-inch square of fusible webbing
- pencil or air-erasable pen
- 4-inch embroidery hoop
- fine beading needle
- matching sewing thread
- 11 purple bugle beads
- purple rocaille beads
- 6 pink diamantés
- 10 pink sequins
- Velcro Coins

1 Apply fusible webbing to one silk square using an iron. Peel off the backing paper, and iron the second silk square on top. Draw the flower in the center of the square with a pencil or air-erasable pen. Stretch the silk in the embroidery hoop.

2 Thread the needle with a double length of thread. Knot the end. Bring the needle to the right side through the center of the silk. Thread on a bugle bead and a rocaille bead. Slide the beads down the thread, and insert the needle back through the bugle bead. Pull the thread taut so the bugle stands upright. Apply the remaining bugles in a cluster around the center.

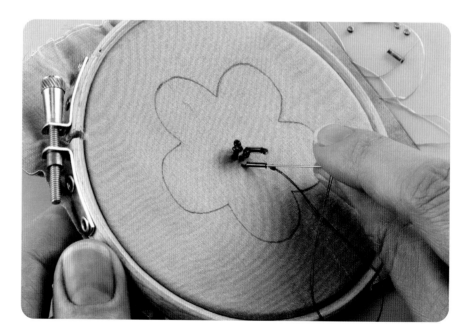

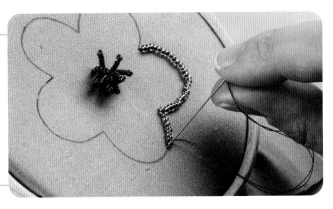

3 Bring the needle to the right side on the flower outline. Thread on four rocaille beads. Lay the beads along the outline, and insert the needle through the silk after the last bead. Make a small backstitch, and insert the needle through the last bead. Thread on four more beads, and continue working the outline.

4 Sew six diamantés around the cluster of bugle beads.

5 Sew the sequins at random on the flower petals, using a single length of thread. Sew a few rocaille beads around the sequins.

6 Remove the silk from the hoop. Carefully cut out the flower around the outline. Attach the flower in place with a Velcro Coin.

Finishing tip

To keep thread ends from trailing out from underneath the flower, stick in place on the underside with fabric glue.

FRINGES & TASSELS

Ornamental and frivolous, tassels and fringes have qualities that have long been exploited by designers producing gorgeous fashion and interior-design accessories. Jazz-age flapper dresses trimmed with rounds of beadwork that swayed as their wearers danced and glass-fringed lampshades are favorite historical examples. More contemporary uses include zipper pulls, key chains, curtain edgings, and chokers.

Stranded fringe

The simplest straight-edged fringe consists of a row of single strands. Each one is made from the same number and type of beads, and they are spaced closely together. By varying the amount of beads, and therefore the length, you can go on to make more decorative zigzag edgings, and geometric patterns can be created within the fringe by changing the color and shape of the beads.

1 To make a strand, fasten the thread securely to the wrong side of the fabric and bring the needle out at the fold or edge. Add on the desired number of beads, then add one or three beads to make the stopper. Thread the needle back up the strand so that the stopper beads are caught in a loop of thread, then take it through the fabric at the point from which it emerged. Start the next strand one bead's width along and continue to the end.

Looped fringe

Looped fringes can also be uniform, but for a different look, try alternating the color of the beads. The third organza bag in the following project has an iridescent shell at the end of each loop: a larger round or faceted bead would also provide additional interest.

1 To make a loop, take the needle and thread through the edge of the fabric. Thread on an odd number of beads—the more beads, the longer the loop will be. Pass the needle back through the fabric so that the last bead sits next to the first. Repeat to the end and fasten securely.

Lattice fringe

A basic off-loom weave is used to make this open diamond edging. At first glance, the instructions may look a little daunting, but if you refer back to the picture, everything will fall into place. Once mastered, this technique could be developed to explore a range of ideas. Try replacing the straight lines of the bugles with a series of rocailles or adding drop beads to the outside edge.

Row ❶ Thread on a rocaille, a small round bead, a rocaille, and a long bugle. Repeat twice and finish off with a rocaille, a round bead, and another rocaille.

Row ❷ Take the needle back through the round bead, and add a rocaille, a bugle, a rocaille, a round bead, a rocaille, a bugle, and a rocaille. Take the needle through the second round bead of row 1, then thread on a rocaille, a bugle, a rocaille, a round bead, and a rocaille. Make a small stitch into the fabric, a short distance along.

Row ❸ Go through the rocaille and round bead, then thread on a rocaille, a bugle, a rocaille, a round bead, a rocaille, a bugle, and a rocaille. Go through the third round bead of row 2, then add a rocaille, a bugle, a rocaille, a round bead, and a rocaille. Repeat rows 2 and 3 to end.

Looped tassel

A narrow color palette of dark plums and browns emphasizes the shape and texture of the beads used for this simple tassel. The large beads are added to the loops at random.

Use these tassels to decorate tab-top curtains, as a key chain, or to hang around a lampshade that is in need of brightening up.

❶ Thread a fine needle with a long double length of strong thread. Secure the end to a large jump ring, then pass the needle through two large beads, and thread on approximately 4 inches of rocailles or other small beads. Take the needle back up through the large beads and over the jump ring to complete the first loop, then repeat to make another nine loops. Fasten the thread back on the jump ring: applying glue over the threads will make it secure.

Gift Bags

The French call these party favor bags *bonbonieres* after the sweets inside. Fill yours with presents, sugared almonds for a wedding, or sweet-smelling lavender, potpourri, or other small treasures as a gift.

YOU WILL NEED:

- 10-inch length of wide organza ribbon or a 4 x 12-inch strip of translucent fabric
- dressmaker's pins
- fine beading needle
- matching thread
- pinking shears
- selection of tiny shells, and rocaille, bugle, round, and drop beads in toning colors
- 4-inch decorative braid (optional)
- 8-inch fine ribbon
- scissors

Each bag requires a selection of approximately 10 grams of beads.

1 Fold the ribbon in half and pin the sides. Work tiny running stitches along each edge, then trim the top with pinking shears. For this looped edging, first stitch a length of braid along the fold. Fasten the thread to a corner, then thread on 5 x 3-mm rocaille beads. Make two small stitches into the braid, ⅓ inch along, and repeat to the end. Work a second row of loops, each of 7 beads, into the same spaces.

2 For a geometric fringe, thread on 3 rocailles, 1 long bugle, and then another 3 rocailles. Add a round bead and 1 rocaille, then bring the needle back through the round bead, and thread on 2 more rocailles, 1 bugle, and 3 rocailles. Secure the V with two small stitches, ½ inch along the fold. Take the needle down through the final rocaille, then repeat to the end, starting each V with 2 rocailles.

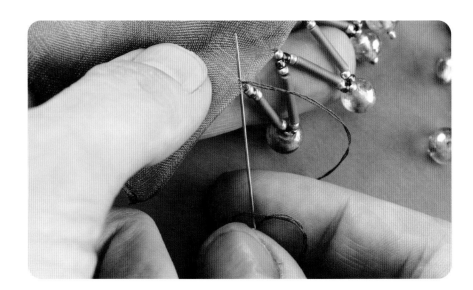

3 Fold the organza in half and sew the sides together by hand or machine, leaving a ½-inch allowance. Trim the seams and top edge with pinking shears, and turn through. For a looped fringe, fasten the thread onto one corner, thread on 15 x 2-mm rocailles, a shell or bead, and another 15 rocailles. Secure with two small stitches, ¼ inch along the crease, and repeat to the end. Trim with narrow braid for a luxurious effect.

4 The second geometric fringe is worked by threading on 1 rocaille, 1 short bugle, 1 rocaille, 1 bugle, 1 rocaille, 1 drop, and 1 rocaille. Take the needle back through the drop and rocaille, and add 1 bugle, 1 rocaille, 1 bugle, and 1 rocaille. Secure the thread ⅓ inch along the fold, take the needle back through the final rocaille, and repeat to the end, starting each V with a bugle.

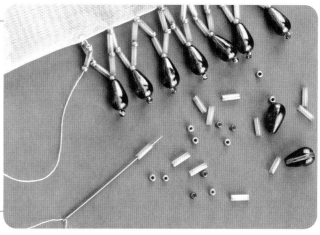

5 To make this single-strand zigzag fringe, start at the corner with a long bugle, a 3-mm rocaille, and three 2-mm rocailles. Take the needle back through the large rocaille and the bugle, and bring it out ⅛ inch along the fold. Add a 3-mm rocaille, then make a strand as before. Make three more strands, each starting with 2, 3, and then 4 rocailles, then three more starting with 3, 2, and then 1 rocaille. Repeat to the end.

6 Extravagant bags need simple ties: to thread a bead onto a fine ribbon, cut the end into tapering points and pass it through the hole. A coat of nail polish may help if the ribbon is very fine. Knot the ribbon and trim off the point.

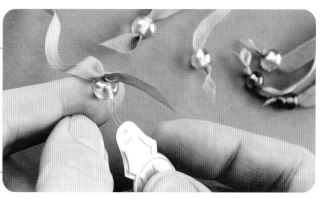

Beaded Bobbles

This fantastic tablecloth will not blow away in a light breeze as outdoor cloths are prone to do. Once you have mastered the art of the bobble making, try using them for other things like key rings and light pulls— once you've started, you won't want to stop.

YOU WILL NEED:

- long sewing needle with large eye
- 80-foot reel of 0.5-mm clear bead elastic
- 30 x 8-mm glass beads for each bobble
- clear glue
- circular tablecloth
- matching sewing thread
- scissors

A 54-inch-diameter cloth requires 32 bobbles.

1 Thread the needle with a 30-inch length of elastic. Following the diagram as you work, thread on beads 1–5, and tie them into a circle close to the end of the elastic. Pass the needle back through the first bead, and add beads 6–9. Take the needle down through the first bead again, through the second bead, and then pull up the elastic to form a second loop of five beads.

 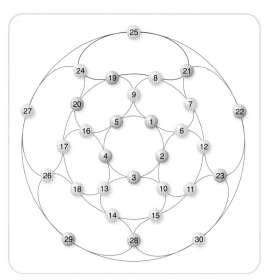

2 Add on beads 10–12, pass the needle through 6, 2, and 3, and draw up to make the third loop. Thread on beads 13–15, take the needle through 10, 3, and 4, and draw up to make the fourth loop. Add 16, 17, and 18, and pass the needle through 13, 4, and 5. Pull up to make the fifth loop.

3   Complete the first half of the ball by threading on
    19 and 20, then taking the needle through 16, 5, 9,
    and 8. Draw up the elastic: the beads will now
form a hemisphere. Thread on 21, 22, and 23, take the needle
back to the left and through 12, 7, 8, and 19, and pull up.

4   Thread on 24 and 25, and pass the needle
    through 21, 8, 19, 20, and 17. Add on 26 and 27,
    and complete the loop by going back through
24, 20, 17, 18, and 14. Thread on 28 and 29, and take the
needle back through 26, 18, 14, 15, 11, and 23.

5   Finish off by adding 30, and passing the needle
    through 29, 27, 25, 22, and back through 30.
    Tighten the final loop by going through 28, and
taking the needle through the beads, back to the knot.
Tie the two ends together tightly, and put a small dab
of glue over the knot. Allow to dry, then clip to ⅛ inch.

6   To mark the positions for the bobbles, fold the
    tablecloth into four and place a pin in the hem
    at each crease line to mark the quarters. Fold
each quarter section into four, and add three more pins
to mark 16 segments, then fold each of these in half
again, giving 32 points around the diameter. Sew a bobble
securely to each point.

Big Crazy Tassel

Never lose your door keys again with this huge tassel. The sophisticated bronze color of the beads would enhance any interior.

YOU WILL NEED:

- 1-inch wooden bead with large holes
- 1-ounce container each of 10-mm twisted bugles, 3-mm rocailles, and 2-mm rocailles
- fine beading needle
- ⅔-inch wooden bead
- 20 x 6-mm round glass beads
- reel of matching Nymo thread
- scissors
- 18 x 6-mm faceted glass beads
- 25 x 10-mm glass drop beads
- 5-inch length of 1-mm wire
- round-nose pliers
- clear glue
- 1 x 8-mm round glass bead

1 To make the tassel head, cover the large wooden bead with the 3-mm rocailles and the small wooden bead with the small rocailles, following the technique given on page 174.

2 Thread 12 round glass beads onto a 12-inch length of Nymo thread. Knot the ends together, then pass the needle several times through the beads to make a firm ring. Knot the ends again, and clip the thread close to the beads.

3 For each strand, cut a 20-inch length of Nymo thread. Make a stopper by threading on 3 small rocailles, then rethread both ends of the thread through the needle. Add a drop bead, a large rocaille, a 6-mm glass bead, and a small rocaille. Complete the strand with 6 or 8 bugles, alternating them with small rocailles. Finish off with a rocaille. Make another 24 strands in various lengths.

4 Lay the strands together on a flat surface. Line up all the final beads, pick up the strands, and knot the threads loosely together. Ease the knot close to the beads using the tip of the pliers, and pull up tightly. Make a second knot a little further along. Coat them both with glue and allow to dry.

5 Clip the loose threads to ¼ inch. Make an open loop at one end of the wire, using the pliers. Hook this between the knots, and fasten tightly in place.

6 Pass the other end of the wire through the large covered bead, the ring, and the small covered bead, and finish off with the large glass bead. Put a little glue between the two covered beads, and allow to dry. Clip the end of the wire to ⅓ inch, and bend into a loop with the pliers. Thread a ribbon through the loop, and tie it onto the key.

WEAVING

This versatile technique, ever increasing in popularity, is continually being explored and developed by contemporary designers who produce innovative jewelry and amulet purses. There are two distinct methods of working, each with its own characteristics, both of which are covered here: loom weaving, synonymous with Native American beadwork, which produces flat, geometric-patterned pieces, and the more free-form, off-loom technique, in which interlocking rounds or rows of beads are built up to create a woven tube, fabric, or daisy chain.

OFF-LOOM WEAVING

Needles and threads

Short, flat-eyed needles are used for off-loom weaving, along with strong Nymo thread, which comes in several thicknesses and a range of colors. If you are working in square stitch and wish the finished piece to be more rigid, use a thicker monofilament that passes through the beads without a needle. As with threading, secure any knots with the tiniest bit of clear nail polish or glue.

Right-angle weave

Row ❶ Cut 12 inches of bead thread or use 15 inches of Nymo thread with a needle at each end, and thread on beads 1–4. Pass the bottom thread up through 4, then add beads 5, 6, and 7. Pass the bottom thread up through 7. Repeat until the weave is the correct width for a wider piece, or continue to bead 13 if making the medal ribbon on page 152. Take the top thread through 11 to turn the corner, ready for the next row.

Row ❷ Add 14, 15, and 16 to the right thread, then take the left thread down through 16. Add 17 and 18, then pass the other thread through 8 and 18. Continue, following the chart, to the end of the row, ending with both threads through 22. Repeat these two rows to the end.

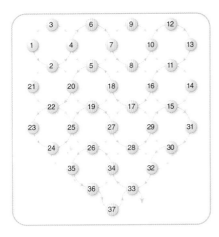

❸ To make a triangular point, follow the chart, reducing the number of beads in each row by two until there is just one bead. The two arrows show the finishing points of the thread. Weave the ends back up the sides to finish off and reinforce the edges, following the previous path.

Interesting effects can be created by using two different-size beads. Each horizontal line is made up of one type to keep the weave even. Just one row makes a quick and simple bracelet or eyeglasses cord. (See the larger diagram on page 153).

Peyote stitch

If worked with large beads, peyote stitch (or honeycomb weave) is solid enough to make mats and coasters, but tiny beads give a quite different and far more delicate effect. It can be flat, as shown here, or woven in the round to make the tubular, spiral jewelry shown on pages 142–145.

The weave is worked in staggered vertical rows, first down and then back up. The diagram shows just a small area of a forget-me-not pattern, so work a small sample first to learn the technique. Extend the repeat downward for a larger piece, or use simple stripes (see below right).

Row ❶ Start at the top left corner and thread beads 1–7. Go back up through 5, add 8, go through 3, add 9, and go through 1.

Row ❷ Thread on 10, go through 9, add 11, go through 8, add 12, and go through 7.

Row ❸ Add 13, go through 12, add 14, go through 11, add 15, go through 10. Repeat rows 2 and 3 to complete.

Thread on beads 1–8, then take the needle back through 1. Add bead 9, then take the needle across the circle and down through 5. Add bead 10, 11, 12, 13, 14, and 15; then go back down through 6. Add 16, and go across and down through 12 to complete the block. Continue according to the diagram, changing the color of the daisies if desired.

Daisy chain

This dainty flower weave is often used for little girls' rings and bracelets. It can be worked in anything from the tiniest delicas, as shown here, to much larger round beads for a chunky look. Use a fine needle and Nymo thread, or elastic for a stretchy bracelet.

Rosette

Weaving in the round, which is working from the center outward, is useful for making small decorative motifs. This rosette could be used singly as an earring, or several could be sewn onto a hair clip, bag, or summer shoe.

You will need 1 × 6-mm center bead, 20 × 3-mm rocailles, and 10 × 4-mm beads. Thread a fine needle with an 8-inch length of fine elastic or monofilament, and make a slipknot at the end.

Round ❶ Thread on the large bead (1) and rocailles 2–6. Take the needle back up through 1, then add rocailles 7–11. Go back up through 1.

Round ❷ Add 12, 13, and 14. Go through 8, then add 15, 16, and 17, and repeat until you are back at 2.

Round ❸ Pass the needle through 7 and 14, then add 27 and go back through 15, 9, and 17. Repeat to the end, then weave the thread back to the center through the beads. Undo the slipknot, and tie the ends tightly together. Clip, then secure with superglue.

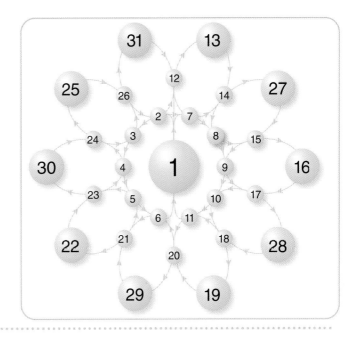

LOOM WEAVING

A bead loom is a simple wire frame across which the warp is threaded and kept under tension. Nymo thread, in a color to blend in with the beads, makes a strong, flexible warp, and long 3-inch beading needles are specially made for weaving. These bend easily and are not easy to use when misshapen, so keep a few spares on hand. The basic technique for setting up and weaving is given in the Loom Bracelet project, on page 132, and can be adapted to any project you may have in mind. The warp always consists of one thread more than the number of beads across the pattern and should be at least 12 inches longer than the finished piece. The width is limited by the width of the loom, but one or more strips can be joined along the edges with slip stitch to create larger weaves. To give an even appearance to the weave, only one size and shape of bead is used in any project. Patterns can be planned on graph paper, with one colored-in square representing one bead: a technique used in the second weaving project, the Fringed Choker, on pages 146–149.

Loom Bracelet

Using a beading loom may seem a daunting task at first, but don't be discouraged. This is the perfect first project for a loom novice and an inspired and fashionable design for a gift or for yourself.

YOU WILL NEED:

- bead loom
- Nymo thread in matching color
- tape measure
- scissors
- needle threader (optional)
- beading needle
- 50 grams of hex beads in approx. 10 different colors
- 2 larger beads for fastening
- clear nail polish (optional)

The finished bracelet measures 7 inches, and the woven part 6¼ inches: adjust the length accordingly to fit a larger or smaller wrist.

1 To set up the loom with a 16-thread warp, 18 inches long, cut 16 x 18-inch lengths of Nymo. Tie together at one end and divide in two. Slip the knot over the pin and spread out the threads so each sits in a groove. Knot the loose ends, fix over the second pin, and separate them. Loosen the wing nut and wind the roller until all the slack has been taken up. Tighten the nut to maintain the tension.

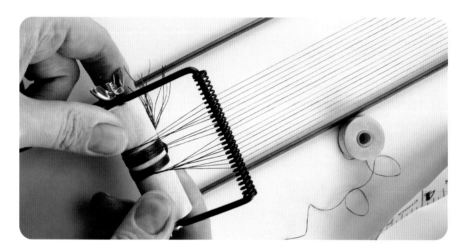

2 Thread the needle with a 24-inch length of Nymo thread, and tie the end to the outer warp thread on the left (or, as here, the right if you are left-handed). Weave a 6¼-inch-long band: for each row, pick up a random selection of 15 hex beads on the needle. Hold these beads under the warp, pushing one up between each thread. Take the needle over the top of the warp and thread back through each bead again, completing one row.

3 Remove the finished piece from the loom by cutting the ends, leaving enough length to knot the warp. Do this by tying a reef knot between each pair of threads. Leaving a pair of threads three beads in from each corner to make the fastenings, sew in the remaining warp ends.

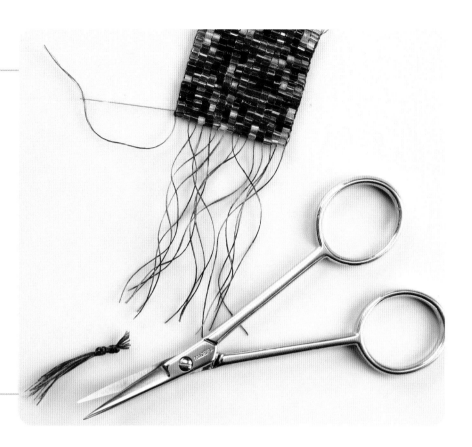

4 For the toggles, thread three hex beads onto one of the remaining pairs of warp threads, then add one large bead and another seed bead. Go back through the large bead and the three small beads. Weave the rest of the thread back into the bracelet, toward the outside edge, then finish off by knotting it to an outer warp and clipping. Make a second toggle at the adjacent corner. To make the loops at the other end, thread 15 seed beads onto a pair of warp threads, and pass the needle back through the first three beads. Check that this fits snugly over the toggle, and adjust as necessary. Finish off as before.

Daisy Necklace

Any young lady would be delighted with this modern pink daisy-chain necklace. The variation has pink bugle beads and clear and pink rocailles, which act as spacers between the daisies.

YOU WILL NEED:

- size 10 beading needle
- fine polyester thread
- 36 x 2-mm pink metallic beads
- 136 x 3-mm diameter white opalescent rocaille beads
- 4-mm-long faceted plastic beads: 9 fuchsia, 8 pale pink, and 56 lilac
- 16 x 6-mm pink glass faceted beads
- 2 small clamshell calottes
- scissors
- silver clasp and jump ring
- small needle-nose pliers

The finished length is approximately 17 inches: add more beads to make a longer necklace.

1 Thread the needle with a 30-inch length of polyester. Knot the ends, then thread on a pink metallic bead. Take the needle back through this bead, 5 inches from the knot. Thread on 1 pink metallic bead, 5 white beads, and 1 fuchsia bead. Pass the needle back down through the first white bead.

2 Add another 3 white beads, then take the needle up through the last white bead before the center. Pull the thread up gently to form the first daisy.

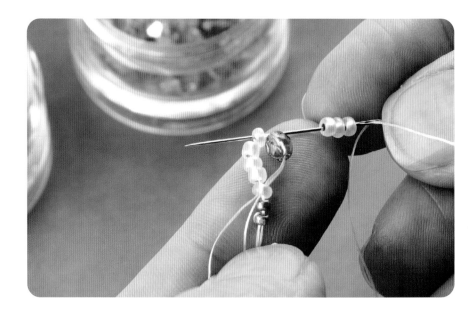

3 Thread 1 pink metallic, 1 lilac, 1 large faceted, 1 lilac, and 1 more pink metallic bead, then 5 white and 1 pale pink bead to begin the next daisy. Take the needle down through the first of the white beads. Continue threading until all the beads have been used, ending with a pink metallic bead.

4 Finish off by fixing on a calotte, using the final pink bead as an anchor. Clip the knot from the other end, and remove the first pink bead. Use this to secure the second calotte. Finish off by fixing the clasp and jump ring to the calottes (see page 61).

Woven Rings

These rings are dripping with fashionable Czech crystals in different tones of the same color. The number of beads used for the ring will vary according to the size desired. However, the finished ring does have some give, so you can experiment with how many are needed.

YOU WILL NEED:

- 28 inches of 3-mm black nylon beading thread
- 15 assorted crystal beads, ranging from 4 mm to 8 mm, in toning shades of mint, teal, and peridot
- 80 x 2-mm green rocaille beads (includes extra for head pins)
- bonding adhesive
- 36 x 4-mm emerald faceted oval beads
- 15 short silver head pins
- wire-cutters
- round-nose pliers
- 6-mm silver jump ring
- flat-nose pliers

1 Start with a 4-mm crystal bead in the center of the nylon thread. Thread on rocailles 2 and 3 to the left, then rocaille 4 and crystal 5 to the right. Pass the left end of the nylon thread through crystal 5 and repeat the process 17 times (see diagram below), ending with rocaille 73. The double row of beads lies around the outside edge and forms the center of the ring. Thread the right end of the nylon through crystal 1, and rocailles 72 and 71 to complete the circle.

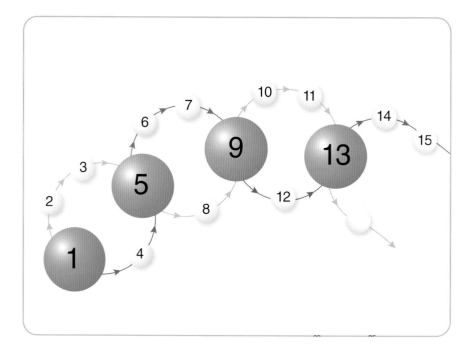

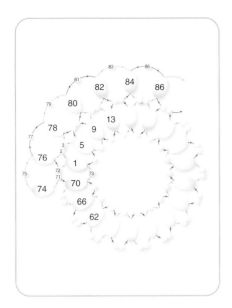

2 To begin the second round, thread crystal 74, rocaille 75, and crystal 76 on the end of the nylon thread that emerges from 71. Take the other end through 76, then add on rocaille 77 and crystal 78. Take the right end through rocailles 2 and 3, then continue threading in this way all around the ring to create a second, interlinked circle (see diagram, left). When the final rocaille has been added, tie the nylon thread in a reef knot (see page 34) at the center of the ring. Clip the ends and make the knot firm with a bit of bonding adhesive.

3 Thread the remaining crystal beads onto the head pins, adding a rocaille after the smaller beads. Use wire-cutters to trim the pins and round-nose pliers to curl over the ends into a loop. Join the pins together in three groups of three and three groups of two.

4 Open the silver jump ring with flat-nosed pliers and attach it to the point in the ring where the threads are knotted, to conceal the join. Thread the six groups of head pins onto the ring, one by one, and close the jump ring firmly. Another drop of glue on the join will help it to remain secure.

Spiral Jewelry

This classic style is timeless in silver and graphite gray. One size of rounded rocaille bead is used throughout, while the woven pattern spirals around to create a tube. A standard bracelet is seven inches, and a choker is sixteen inches: adjust these lengths to fit.

YOU WILL NEED:

- size 10 beading needle
- reel of matching Nymo thread
- rocaille beads
- clear adhesive glue
- scissors
- 2 small jump rings
- crab claw or toggle fastening

Allow 30 grams of rocaille beads for the bracelet, and 50 grams for the necklace.

1 Thread the needle with a 2-yard length of Nymo thread and knot the loose ends. To make the foundation loop, thread on beads 1 to 9, and, leaving a 6-inch tail, tie a reef knot (see page 34).

2 Support the loop by holding the tail between your forefinger and thumb, and maintain tension by wrapping the loose end around the other fingers. Slide the needle back through 1, add on 10, and pass the needle through 3.

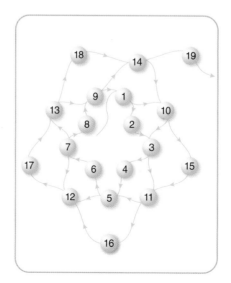

3 To complete the first round, thread on 11, pass the needle through 4; thread on 12, pass the needle through 7; thread on 13, pass the needle through 9. The beads will now form a flat, four-pointed star shape.

4 For the second round, thread on 14, pass the needle through 10; thread on 15, pass the needle through 11; thread on 16, pass the needle through 12; thread on 17, pass the needle through 13. Draw the thread up tightly, the beads will now begin to form a cylinder.

5 The next and subsequent rounds are worked in the same way: continue adding beads in a clockwise spiral to create the desired length. Each new bead will slot neatly into the space in the previous round. As the cylinder lengthens, it becomes easier to handle: hold it between your forefinger and thumb and rotate slowly.

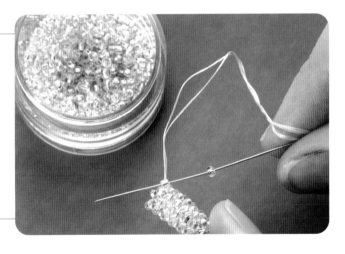

6 To finish off, work the next three beads into every other space to reduce the diameter, then pass the thread once again through the final six beads. Sew one half of the fastener in place by making several overstitches, passing the needle under the last beads, and finally secure with a drop of glue. Cut the knot from the other end and rethread the needle. Finish off in the same way, then sew on the remaining part of the fastener.

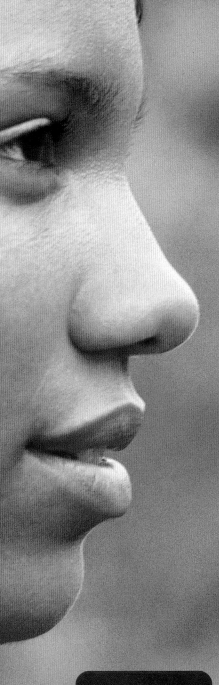

Fringed Choker

This modern woven pattern is bound onto soft leather to tie around the neck. The pattern includes short fringes that can be extended to any length that you want.

YOU WILL NEED:

- bead loom
- tape measure
- Nymo thread
- beading needle
- 30 grams of 2-mm rocaille beads in iridescent red and two shades of turquoise
- scissors
- remnant of matching leather, at least 2 x 24 inches
- white glue
- matching sewing thread
- fine sewing needle

Refer back to the Loom Bracelet on pages 130–133 for instructions on how to set up the loom and the basic weaving technique.

1 Thread the loom with a 20-inch-long warp of eleven strands of Nymo thread, and fasten on the weft. Following the chart, on which one colored square represents one bead, weave the first 28 rows as far as the first strand of the fringe.

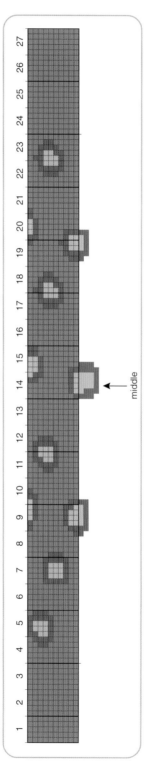

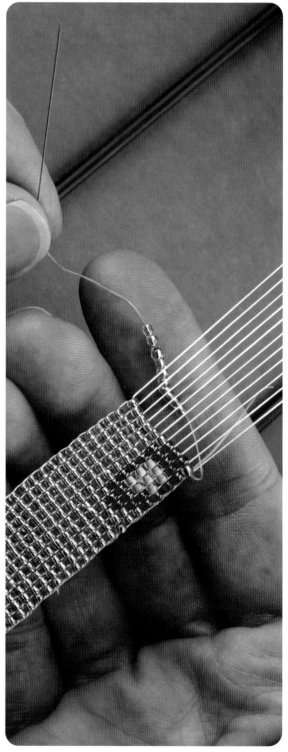

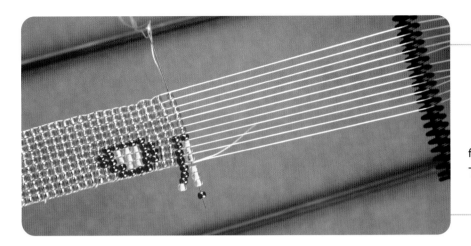

2 To make a strand, thread on the beads as indicated on the chart and push the first ten up into the warp as usual. The rest will extend as the fringe.

3 Pass the needle back through the second bead from the end, through the three loose beads, and then back through the remaining beads.

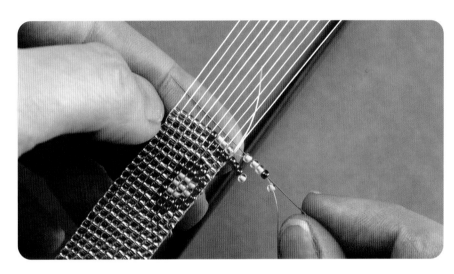

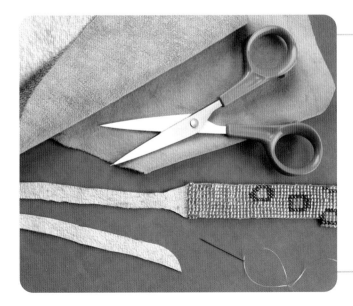

4 Continue to the end of the chart, remove the beading from the loom, and then knot the warp threads in pairs and trim to 1 inch. Cut a strip of leather the same width and 10 inches longer than the beading. Glue the choker to the center of the leather on the right side, tucking the knotted threads neatly under the beads. When dry, slip stitch the four edges of the choker to the leather, then taper the ends to make the ties.

Medals

No heroism is required to win this quirky set of brooches. The off-loom square weaving technique, explained in the techniques section, is used with stripes to emulate the real thing, while each one is finished in a different way. One has a pendant, one tassels, and one a shiny star.

YOU WILL NEED:

for the star medal:
- 20 x 3-mm silver rocailles
- 12 inches fine silver beading wire No. 34
- 10 x 6-mm silver liquid twist bugle beads
- 5 x 4-mm bicone crystal beads in different colors
- 5 grams of 3-mm rocailles in iridescent black and pink
- 1 x ¼-inch (6-mm) jump ring

for the fringed medal:
- 5 grams of 3-mm rocailles in iridescent black, green, bronze, and silver
- 5 x ⅛-inch (4-mm) jump rings
- 5 small silver head pins

for the pendant medal:
- 5 grams of 3-mm rocailles in iridescent black, silver, and mauve
- black faceted drop bead
- ⅛-inch (4-mm) jump ring
- decorative silver bail

for all the medals:
- wire-cutters
- sewing needle
- nylon beading thread
- ⅔-inch brooch backing
- round-nose pliers

1 The "ribbons" are all made with a square off-loom weave, following the technique steps on page 127. For the star medal, work in vertical black and pink stripes: weave 6 rows, then taper the end to a point as shown on the diagram opposite. Weave the loose ends back up through the sides, following the path of the threads, and finish off with a knot at the center top.

2 To make the star, thread 4 silver rocaille beads onto the center of a 12-inch length of silver beading wire. Pass the right end of the wire back through the first bead and pull up, then add a bugle and a crystal bead to each end. Pass the right end of the wire through the crystal on the left to form the first point.

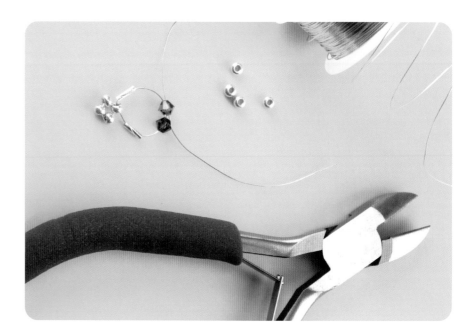

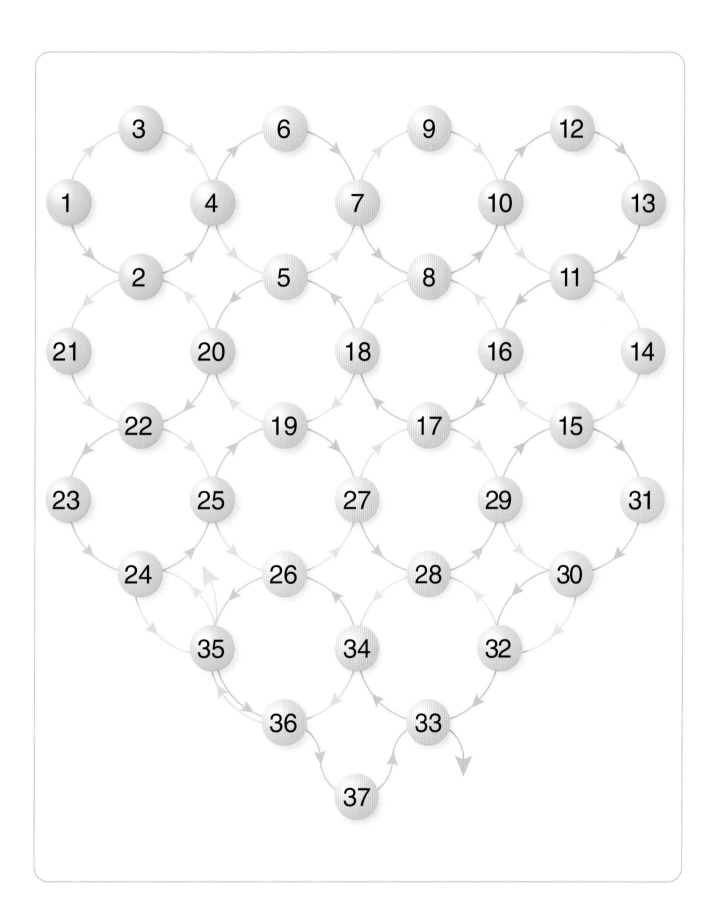

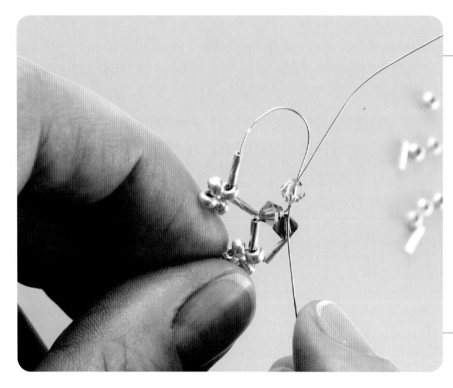

3 Thread a bugle and four rocailles onto the left wire. Pass the end back through the first rocaille and gently pull the loop up. Add another bugle and the third crystal, then pass the other end of the wire up through the crystal to complete the second point.

4 Make three more points in the same way. Finish the star by passing the working wire back through the first bead. Twist the two ends securely together, then clip them with wire-cutters. Open a ¼-inch (6-mm) jump ring, and fix it to the center of the star, between two points, then fix the star to the point of its ribbon. Sew a brooch backing to the top edge with clear nylon thread.

5 The ribbon for the fringed medal is worked in stripes of black, green, bronze, and silver, as shown. Leaving a straight lower edge, fix a jump ring to each of the five beads along this edge. Thread 5 rocailles onto a head pin, trim the top to ¼ inch with wire-cutters, and then bend into a loop and secure to the first ring. Put 6 beads on the next wire, 7 on the center, and then 6 and 5 beads, in turn.

6 The pendant medal has a ribbon made as for step 1, with a central stripe of silver beads and a band of black on one side and mauve on the other. Fix the brooch backing to the top edge, then use a small jump ring to fix a bail to the point. Close the bail over the hole at the top of the black drop bead.

KNOTTING & CROCHET

Crochet and macramé may have been sidelined in recent years, but as with everything else, craft styles turn full circle, and these 1970s favorites are once again the height of fashion.

Knotting

Single knots provide space between threaded beads, either separating them in a functional way or throwing them into focus—as with a beaded curtain or the Collector's Necklace on pages 168–171. Rows of knots, however, will turn a string of beads into a macramé bracelet or even (for the nostalgic) a hanging plant container.

Bead curtain

An all-glass bead curtain makes a stunning screen for a small window. Thread the beads onto a fine cord or leather thong, spacing them at intervals and keeping them in place with a single overhand knot. Hang the strands from a length of wooden batten, and screw it to the top of the frame or recess: see step 5 of the Beaded Curtain, on pages 184–187, for instructions.

Flat knot weave

The basic macramé flat knot can be worked in string with handmade beads to make a surfer-style bracelet, or with embroidery twist and small glass beads for a more delicate look.

❶ Tie two lengths of yarn or string together with an overhand knot, one third of the way down their length. Pin the loop to the working surface, and thread a bead onto the two shorter strands. To make the first part of the knot, lay the long thread on the left across the two center strands at a right angle. Pass the right thread below this and behind the two center strands, then bring it out through the loop on the left. Pull up gently.

❷ Take the left strand behind the center strands at a right angle, and pass the right strand below it, over the center strands and through the loop on the left. Repeat to the end. Make a final loop that will catch over the first bead as a closure, or use the yarn to tie off on the wrist.

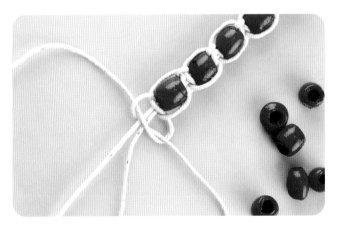

Crochet

Glass or wooden beads will add color and texture to any crocheted project, from a simple rectangular purse to a trim along the edges of a scarf. As opposed to knotting, where the beads are added as you go, all the beads for a crocheted piece have to be threaded on at the beginning. They will appear on the wrong side of the finished piece, and so are incorporated into every alternate row on a square piece, or on each round of a circular or cylindrical piece, such as the Wastepaper Basket on pages 160–163. Small beads can be incorporated into a short stitch, such as single crochet, but bigger beads need a longer stitch to accommodate their height.

Incorporating a bead

Push the bead down the thread just before the yarn is pulled through for the final stage of the stitch: here, for a half-double, the hook is about to go through the three loops, and the bead will sit at the back of the finished stitch.

Abbreviations

ch	= chain
sl st	= slip stitch
sc	= single crochet
dc	= double crochet
hdc	= half double crochet

Pitcher cover

Beaded muslin pitcher covers are both decorative and practical, and they were once to be found in every pantry, protecting the milk from possible insect attacks. Large-holed glass beads, often known as "jug beads," were added to a simple crochet border to make the weighted edging.

Start with a 6-inch-diameter circle of fine fabric, and tack under a ⅛-inch hem. Thread on the beads, allowing 1 bead for each ⅓ inch of the diameter, plus a few spares.

Round ❶ Using a 6 steel (1.5 mm) hook and No. 20 thread, work sc all around the muslin to conceal the raw edges.

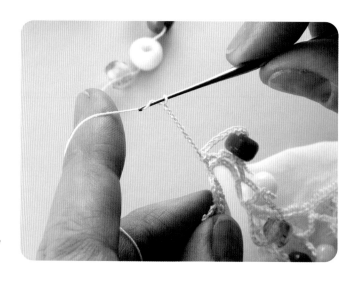

Round ② 2 8 ch, skip 4, 1sc to end. Vary the spaces between the last few loops, as necessary, to fit the number of stitches in round 1. Then 4 sl st into first 4 ch.

Round ③ 3 14 ch. Remove hook from loop, and slide a bead down.

Reinsert the hook, then 1 sc over center of next loop to end. Then 1 sl st into first sc, and finish off.

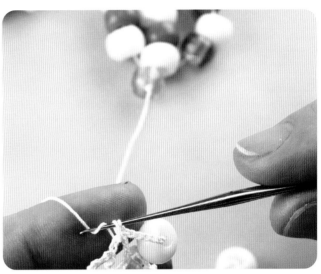

How to thread the beads

Coaxing a thick, fraying thread through beads is not easy, but this old-fashioned tip makes the task a cinch: Thread a needle with sewing thread, and knot the ends. Pass the last 6 inches of the yarn through the loop, then thread the beads onto the needle and pass them down the cotton and onto the yarn.

Wastepaper Basket

By incorporating alternating colors of large wooden beads into a striped pattern of red, orange, and natural twines using single crochet, this wastepaper basket has a homespun quality that could easily blend into many interiors. The beads are threaded onto the colored twine and added in as the basket is crocheted. This project uses a basic crochet stitch, but make sure you read and understand the instructions before proceeding.

YOU WILL NEED:

- size J/10 (6-mm) crochet hook
- 1 x 1-lb. ball natural garden twine
- 1 x 5-oz. ball dyed jute twine in each color of red, dark orange, and light orange
- large-eyed sewing needle
- 84 assorted wooden beads in natural, pink, orange, and red

finished height: 10 inches

1 Using the natural twine, chain five stitches; join together with a slip stitch. Single crochet twice into every stitch, and place a colored string for a marker at the join. Work single crochet stitch once into every stitch; from then on, increase in every other row. Work single crochet throughout. Make the increases by first increasing every other stitch by one stitch, then the next increase row every third stitch, the next increase row every fourth stitch, etc. This will keep the disk shape enlarging evenly and flatly.

2 Crochet the base to 9½ inches across. Place a marker at the finishing point. Begin the sides by crocheting one single crochet into every stitch along the edge. Turn the work so that the crochet hook faces you and work in the opposite direction to which the base is worked. Make five rows in single crochet and cut off, leaving a tail.

3 Take the ball of red twine and string 12 beads in two alternating colors onto the twine. Attach to the tail of the natural twine and continue the sides using single crochet, following the pattern below. For the beaded rows, work a bead into every sixth stitch by drawing up one bead and making a stitch behind it.

- 3 rows red—bead the middle row
- I row light orange
- I row natural
- I row dark orange—bead row
- I row natural
- I row light orange
- 3 rows red—bead the middle row
- 3 rows natural

4 Repeat the pattern. Finish off the top edge by crocheting a slip stitch around the rim. Cut off and work in the end.

Napkin Rings

Pearls never go out of fashion, but if you don't like wearing yours, let them enhance your table. Crochet in colored wire or classic copper.

YOU WILL NEED:

- 40 pearls in assorted sizes
- 9 yards flexible colored wire
- size E/4 (3.5-mm) crochet hook
- wire-cutters
- snipe-nose pliers

1 Thread the beads onto the wire. Hold the wire 2 inches from the end and make a loop by wrapping the main wire over this short end and pulling it through with the hook. Pull both ends to tighten. Work a foundation of 25 chain stitches: each stitch is worked by wrapping the hook under and then over the wire and pulling the wire through the loop on the hook to form a new loop. Join the ring with a slip stitch: insert the hook through the first loop and pull the wire through.

2 The napkin ring is worked with three rounds of double crochet. Work another three chain, then wrap the wire around the hook. Insert it under the top two loops of the second chain and draw the wire through the chain so that there are now three loops on the hook.

3 Wrap the wire around the hook and draw the hook through the first two loops. There are now two loops on the hook: wrap the wire around the hook once more and draw it through these to make one double crochet stitch.

4 Work one double crochet into each chain, incorporating the pearls into the stitches by sliding them, one at a time, down the wire so that they lie on the outside. Space them irregularly to create a random look. Finish the round by working a slip stitch into the top of the first stitch. Work another two rounds in the same way. To complete the ring, clip the end of the wire and finish off by weaving both loose ends into the crochet. Use the pliers to neaten them so that there are no sharp ends.

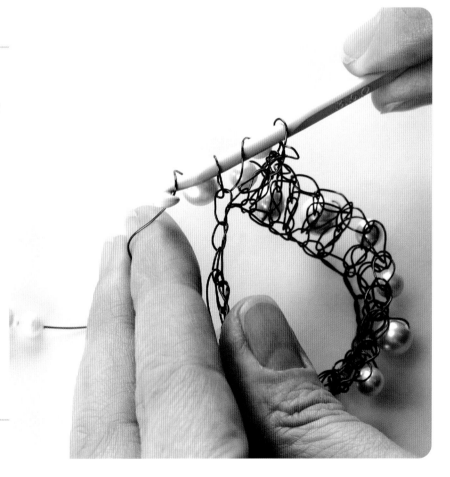

Collector's Necklace

This is the project that uses up all those beads that you have been hoarding and shows off the more distinctive and unique styles. Heavy silk thread is knotted to hold the individual beads in place and becomes a feature of the finished piece.

YOU WILL NEED:

- approximately 70 beads in various sizes
- necklace planning tray (optional)
- 3¾ yards heavy silk twist thread
- 1 two-holed button
- tapestry needle
- stranded embroidery thread to match
- scissors

1 Arrange the beads in two rows, using a planning tray if desired. Thread the silk through the holes in the button to make it into a toggle. Slide the button down to halfway along the thread, and secure by tying both ends together with a simple overhand knot. Thread the first bead onto one of the strands, then knot the silk again, leaving a space of about ¼ inch.

2 Continue threading the beads, some singly and some in groups of three, until the necklace measures approximately 18 inches. To make the loop end of the fastening, tie the silk into a slipknot, ensuring that it is big enough to pass easily over the button.

3 Knot the second strand of beads in the same way until it is 1½ inches longer (or shorter, depending on the number of beads) than the first, and tie it firmly to the stem of the button fastening. Trim the ends.

4 Thread the tapestry needle with a 20-inch length of stranded thread, and work a round of buttonhole stitches around the silk loop. Finish off the ends by sliding the needle under the stitches. Reinforce the stem of the toggle in the same way.

BEADS & EMBELLISHMENTS

It could easily be argued that beads are embellishments in themselves, but for those who can't resist additional ornament, there are endless ways to fashion the tiniest seed beads and sequins into gorgeous little fripperies: buttons, tassels, baubles, and even beads that have been covered with a layer of beads.

Pin beading

Polystyrene craft forms come in various sizes and shapes, from teddy bears to circlets, hearts, and fruits. Simple round balls studded with colored beads or sequins make great ornaments to hang from the Christmas tree or just pile high in a pretty bowl. You should use special short beading pins that measure no more than ½ inch, since dressmaker's pins will become entangled within the polystyrene. Thread a rocaille bead, then a sequin onto the pin and push it into the form. Repeat until the entire ball is covered, overlapping the sequins so that no white shows through. Flat sequins will give a smoother finish than cup sequins, but both are equally effective.

Beaded button

Fix one of these lovely candylike buttons to a clip-on earring backing, or sew a line of them as a spectacular finish for a special cushion cover or even a jacket.

Cover a self-cover button with toning fabric, following the manufacturer's instructions carefully. Fasten the thread to the center. Sew on small beads, one at a time, as close together as you can manage, until all of the background is concealed. Work in a circular fashion from the middle outward.

Beaded bead

A single beaded bead is perfect as a decorative head for a tassel (see also the Big Crazy Tassel, on pages 122–125) or used on its own as an earring, but imagine the impact of a whole row, graded in size and color and threaded into a long necklace. Choose a foundation bead of a tone similar to the small beads, and a matching thread.

1 Take the thread through the large bead, tie the ends together, and secure the knot just inside the hole with a blob of clear glue to prevent it from slipping. Thread on enough seed beads to lie comfortably around the side of the bead without leaving space at either end, then take the needle back through the hole. Pass it back through the first two beads, then add two less than the number of beads in the first row. Go through the last two beads and back through the large bead. Repeat this row to make the first "orange segment."

2 Continue making segments of three rows to cover the whole bead, then finish off the thread securely, and trim the ends. Vary the effect by alternating the colors of the beads in each row.

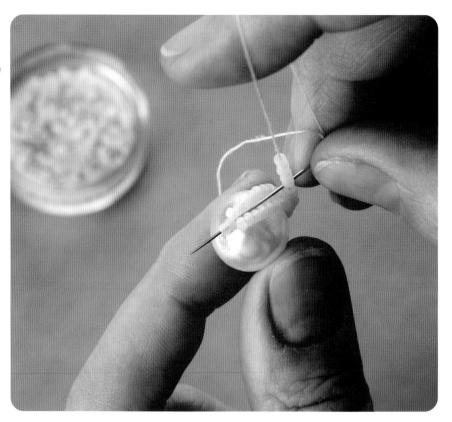

Polymer clay beads

Polymer clay is readily available from craft suppliers under various brand names. It is clean and easy to use, comes in many colors, and can be blended for subtly marbled effects. Children (under supervision!) love using it for its immediacy and simplicity, but for the more patient, it can also be used to make intricate mosaics and imitations of Venetian millefiori: see the funky beads of the Millefiori bracelet on pages 180–183.

❶ Small-scale cutters can be used to cut shapes from rolled-out clay.

❷ Turn flat shapes into pendants by pushing a cut-off eye pin into the top before baking.

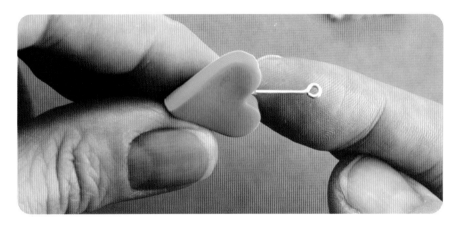

❸ To make these marbled beads, simply knead small amounts of different colors together, then break off pea-sized lumps, and roll into balls between the palms. Pierce by threading each ball onto thick wire and gently twisting them around to enlarge the holes.

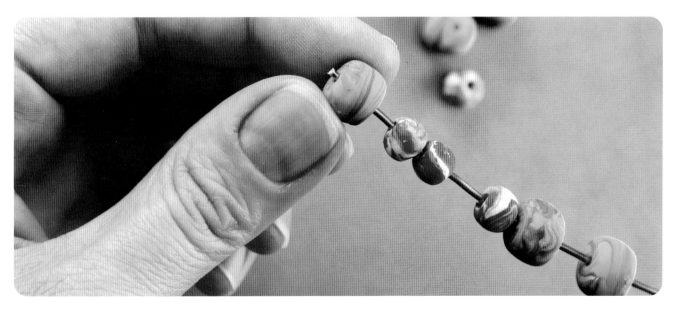

Beaded Fruits

These exquisite beaded fruits can grace the table for months on end. All that is required is a blow from a hair dryer from time to time to remove the dust. Use silk fruits, rather than polystyrene foam, available from florist's suppliers and craft stores, because they are a better shape and have realistic stalks, which add the finishing touch. The technique is easy: just thread a small seed bead onto a short beading pin, add a sequin, and then press the pin into the fruit shape.

YOU WILL NEED:

- silk fruits
- brass sequin and bead pins
- selection of seed beads
- cup sequins

Allow 1 package of pins, 50 grams of seed beads, and 10 grams of sequins per fruit.

1 Choose a selection of beads and sequins to match the color of the fruit. For the lemon, use clear and solid yellow beads, with a few cream and green beads to add depth. For the pear, choose crystal and gold-colored sequins. On the pin, pick up a bead and then a sequin.

2 Press the pin into the fruit. It may be easier to use a thimble. Each sequin should overlap the last slightly. As the fruits are already colored, small gaps between the sequins will not be noticeable.

3 Select beads and sequins in a random fashion using mainly crystal sequins to give the fruits a translucent appearance. Continue adding beads and sequins until the fruit is completely covered.

4 Make five or six different fruits to create an attractive group in a dish.

ADVANCED

Millefiori Bracelet

These fabulous beads echo the beautiful Venetian Murano glass beads that are made with different-colored glass rods that resemble a thousand flowers, *mille fiori*.

YOU WILL NEED:

- 1 package each of polymer clay in at least 5 different colors
- fine craft blade
- small rolling pin or bead drum
- kebab sticks or fine knitting needles
- 12-inch matching cord
- matching sewing thread
- sewing needle

1 To make the core, roll a small piece of clay into a sausage shape, approximately ⅕ inch in diameter and 1¼ inch long. For the next round, cut a ⅛-inch slice each of two contrasting colors. Cut each slice into four ⅛-inch strips, then arrange them alternately to form stripes. Press them together, roll lightly, and then wrap around the core so the stripes are horizontal.

2 Roll out a sheet of a third color, just big enough to wrap over the stripes, then roll the sausage gently and evenly with your fingertips until it is about ⅓ inch in diameter. The smaller the roll, the finer the millefiori will be.

3 Make the main bead from a fourth color, rolling the clay between your palms to form a round ball. Gently push the stick or knitting needle through the center to make a hole, then slide off the bead.

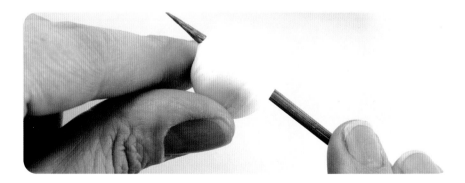

4   Cut paper-thin slices from the clay roll, and carefully press each one onto the bead, leaving space all around. When it is completely covered, roll the bead until the surface is smooth and the joins have disappeared. Repierce the hole. Make several more beads—a total of eight or nine should be enough for the average wrist—then bake them according to the manufacturer's instructions.

5   There are infinite variations on this basic millefiori pattern. Try omitting the third color and fixing the slices onto a contrasting bead; arrange them so that no background color is visible, or with extra layers of clay to make concentric circles.

6   Set aside the smallest bead. Starting 2 inches from the end, thread the other beads onto the cord, separating each one with a knot (see page 35).

7   Thread on the last bead, then make it into a toggle by tying the end of the cord around the final knot. Trim the end, then secure with a few stitches.

8   Fold the other end of the cord into a loop. Make sure that it will slip over the toggle, then knot the end. Pass the end through the first bead, trim, and again stitch it in place.

Beaded Curtain

Keep out unwanted visitors with this groovy curtain inspired by insect screens. The beads are handmade from Japanese origami paper that has been rolled up and artificial flowers culled from various sources.

YOU WILL NEED:

- hacksaw
- wooden batten
- acrylic paint
- paintbrush
- 1 package origami paper in various patterns
- scissors
- 1 package garden sticks
- plastic wrap
- white glue
- strong thread
- approx. 100 x 8-mm colored plastic beads
- crewel needle
- plastic drinking straws
- silk flower heads

1 Saw the batten ¾ inch narrower than the width of the door frame. Paint the batten, and leave to dry. Cut triangles of origami paper 6 inches long with a 1½-inch-wide base.

2 Wrap garden sticks with plastic wrap. This will prevent the paper beads from adhering to the sticks. Starting at their bases, wrap the triangles tightly around the sticks, brushing with white glue as you work. Apply a final coat of white glue as a varnish. Leave to dry, then slip the beads off the sticks. Pull out the plastic wrap.

3 Cut a length of strong thread twice the height of the curtain, plus another 16 inches. Slide a plastic bead onto the thread. Adjust the bead to sit in the middle of the thread. Pass both ends through a crewel needle. Cut plastic drinking straws to 1⅜ inch long to use as spacers. Thread on a spacer.

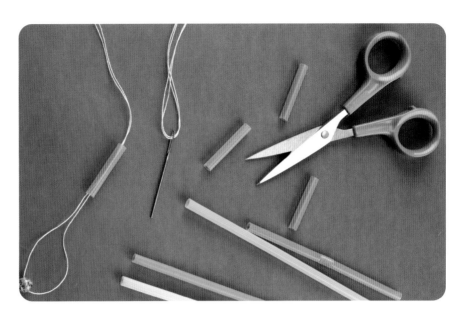

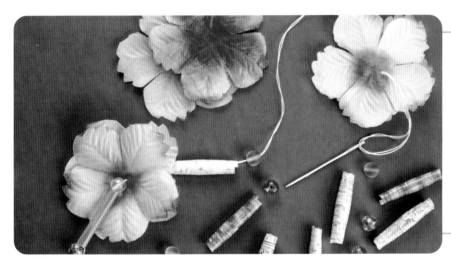

4 Slide on another plastic bead. Thread on two silk flower heads and another plastic bead. Next, string on a paper bead, a plastic bead, and so on. Continue adding flower heads, beads, and spacers until you are happy with the length. Make enough bead strings for the batten.

5 Drill a row of holes along the batten for the strings. Thread the strings up through the batten, and knot the ends securely above the batten. Cut off the excess.

SUPPLIERS

The Internet is now a truly global marketplace. An enormous range of suppliers, both retail and wholesale, can deliver every imaginable kind of bead directly to your doorstep. These are just a few of the best and the most unusual Web sites:

www.affordablebeading.com
a wide selection of beads, findings, thread, and cords, all with no minimum order

www.allseedbeads.com
as you would expect, every type of Czech seed bead conceivable

www.beadbazaar.co.nz
ideas on how to make jewelry, as well as a huge range of beads, including clay, paua shell, and wood

www.bead-world.com
huge selection, including Japanese delicas and Venetian glass

www.brightlingsbeads.com
good selection, including sterling findings, glass beads, Swarovski crystal, and freshwater pearls

www.brucefrankbeads.com
unusual antique and contemporary beads including ancient collector beads

www.ebeadshop.com
wholesale and retail beaders with a constant supply of new items

www.honeybeads.com
wide range of special beads, including Czech glass, lampwork, and gold- or silver-filled beads

www.indiabead.com
Indian beads directly from the makers

www.jewelrysupply.com
comprehensive selection, including magical magnetic beads and beads from around the world

www.londonbeadco.co.uk
embroidery and yarn supplies and hundreds of beads of all kinds

www.matoska.com
comprehensive selection of glass beads for use in Native American and other craft projects, including antique trade beads

www.shipwreck.com
wide-ranging selection—the world's largest—of beads, findings, and related materials

www.thebeadsite.com
the definitive reference point for anyone interested in the cultural significance of beads: the online site for the Centre for Bead Research, set up by the late Peter Francis Jr.

www.venetianbeadshop.com
unique site from a family-owned business working directly with Murano and Venetian beadmakers

www.2bead.com
a great source of inspiration

Bibliography

Cassell's Compendium of Victorian Crafts. Marjorie Henderson and Elizabeth Wilkinson. Cassell, 1977.

The Complete Book of Beads. Janet Coles and Robert Budwig. Dorling Kindersley, 1990.

Costume Jewelry in Vogue. Jane Mulvagh. Thames and Hudson, 1988.

Embroidery with Beads. Angela Thompson. Batsford, 1987.

The Essential Guide to Embroidery. Ed. Karen Hemingway. Murdoch Books, 2002.

Fortuny. Guillermo de Osma. Aurum Press, 1980.

The Native Americans. Ed. Colin F. Taylor. Salamander, 1991.

On Women and Friendship. Starr Ockenga Stewart. Tabori and Chang, 1993.

Spangles and Superstitions. Written and published by Christine & David Springett, 1987.

Venetian Color. Paul Hills. Yale, 1999.

ACKNOWLEDGMENTS

The author

I have enjoyed writing and making projects for this book tremendously, and have worked alongside some very creative people. The final product is very much a joint effort and could not have been possible without the combined talents of the team at MQ Publications. Thank you to everybody, and especially to Ljiljana, for asking me to write it in the first place; Katy for your inspiration, constant support and unswerving faith that we'd get it all together, with Sorrel's help; Lizzie, for taking the fantastic photos, and Catherine, for styling them so beautifully; Cheryl, Akemi, Lindsay, Karin, and Dorothy, for contributing such individual projects; to my friends Sarah, Emma, and Ingrid, for lending me their South African bead jewelry; and to my family, as ever. I am also indebted to the London Bead Co./Delicate Stitches, who supplied many of the beads and materials.

The makers:

Katy Bevan
Blossom
Lucinda Ganderton
Light Pull, Multistrand Necklace, Floating Necklace, Choker and Bracelet, Vintage Earrings, Charm Bracelet, Crystal Hearts, Lilac Corsage, Beads and Buttons Bag, Brocade Cushion Cover, Gift Bags, Beaded Bobble Cloth, Big Crazy Tassel, Daisy Necklace, Spiral Necklace and Bracelet, Napkin Rings, Collector's Necklace, Millefiori Bracelet
Karin Hossack
Wastepaper Basket
Lindsay Kaubi
Chandelier, Simple Loomed Bracelet, Fringed Choker
Cheryl Owen
Spiky Brooch, Appliqué Blooms, Eastern Flower Curtain
Akemi Sugawara
Lariat, Woven Rings, Off-Loom Medals
Dorothy Wood
Beaded Fruits

The suppliers

Thank you to the following companies who loaned props for the shoot:

After Noah
020 73594281 www.afternoah.biz
London Furniture Company
020 78810160
www.londonfurniturecompany.co.uk
Graham and Green
www.grahamandgreen.co.uk
Missoni Home at Interdesign
020 73765272
www.interdesignuk.com
Muji 020 73232208
www.muji.co.uk
Lucy in the Sky 020 73511577
The Lavender Room 01273 220380

Picture credits:

Diagrams: Anthony Duke. Page 5: Aprosio, Florence, Italy (www.aprosio.it). Page 11: The Art Archive/Dagli Orti. Page 12: The Art Archive/Staatliche Sammlung Ägyptischer Kunst, Munich/Dagli Orti. Page 13: The Art Archive/Museo de America, Madrid/Dagli Orti. Page 14: © Peter Bowater/Alamy. Page 15: ©1998 Hollingsworth Studios, Inc. Page 17: Steve Wood/Rex Features.

INDEX

Nymo thread 24

O

off-loom weaving 127–9
overlapping sequins 97

P

pearls 10, 17, 20
    napkin rings 79, 164–7
peyote stitch 128
pins 22, 28
    eye pins 22, 62, 63
    head pins 22, 37, 62
    pin beading 173
    safety pin bracelets 36
    wire pins 62
pitcher cover 158–9
pliers 28
Poiret, Paul 17
polymer clay beads 175
power bracelets 14
prayer beads 10, 15

R

reef knots 34
ribbon 24
    gift bags 37, 114–17
right angle weave 127
ring 138–41
rocailles 20
rope necklace 37
rosary beads 10, 15
rosette 129

S

safety pin bracelets 36
satin stitch 95
Schiaparelli, Elsa 17
scissors 28
sequins 20
    sequins and beads 97
sewing on different surfaces 96
sewing single beads 95
silk cord 24
South America 10, 13
spacing beads 34
    beaded curtain 37, 157, 184–7
spiral jewelry 142–5
status symbols 10
Swarovski, Daniel 13

T

tassels 110–13
    big crazy tassel 122–5
threading 32–7, 159
    needle threaders 28
    Nymo thread 24
threads 24–5
    thread conditioner 28
tigertail 26, 76, 79
    bead choker and bracelet 37, 52–5, 79
tokens of affection 15
tools 28–9
trade beads 13, 15
triangular links 22, 63
Turkey 10

tying reef knots 34

V

Venetian glass 11, 12–13
Victorians 16, 17
vintage earrings 64–7

W

wampum 15
wastepaper basket 160–3
weaving 126–9
wire 26–7
wire beading 76–9
wire binding 78–9
    crimped bead choker and bracelet 37, 52–5
    crystal hearts 80–3
    lariat 37, 44–7
    light pull 38–9
    pearly napkin rings 164–7
wire cutters 28
wired beads 77
wire pins 62
wire rings 22
wound beads 12
woven ring 138–41
wrapping 78